Good News about Gender is a tre[...] groups, Sunday School classes, a[...] word speaks to our embodimen[...] body of Christ and to serve the [...] community, and calling. In eacl[...]

M000306102

engage Scripture with thoughtful exegetical and hermeneutical methods, and pray and talk together. Questions of gender identity, men's and women's roles, and responsibilities in church and mission continue to be centrally important for Christians and their churches. This resource will be a blessing to all who wish to dig deeper into what God's Word says to us about our bodies, our relationships, our identities, and our calling to serve God in the world."

— Dr. Jenell Paris, Professor of Anthropology, Messiah College (Grantham, PA), author of *The End of Sexual Identity: Why Sex is too Important to Define Who We Are.*

"What I love about Rasmussen's work is that it's both authentic and smart. Authentic in that it flows from her own life-story and incredible passion for gender issues. Smart in that she's able to guide her readers through some challenging theological and exegetical questions like an old pro, belying her age. Study groups will strike gold in these pages as they dig through the biblical material and respond with the creative exercises provided."

—Rick Mattson, author of *Faith is Like Skydiving: And Other Memorable Images for Dialogue with Seekers and Skeptics.*

"A fresh voice, biblically rich, culturally broad, practically applicable. Here is a guide for girls and women everywhere, to help us grow to be the blessings that God created us to be."

—Miriam Adeney, PhD, Associate Professor of World Christian Studies Seattle Pacific University, author, of *Kingdom Without Borders: The Untold Story of Global Christianity*

"In many respects, this is a groundbreaking Bible Study Guide. The layout and content are highly interactive and engaging; the direct and simple writing style makes it very easy for readers to follow along whether in groups or individually. The author's abundant use of real-life practical examples with tips for further exploration helps not only to drive home learning points, but also to make Bible study a fun and interesting experience. This Study Guide goes straight to the nitty-gritty issues surrounding gender identity and relationships in a manner that is culturally sensitive, yet forthright and challenging. We live in a country where cultural ideals about what it means to be male and female are taught as biblical commands, just as Rasmussen infers. The damaging results are evident in wounded hearts, stunted lives, unhappy homes and failed marriages. Therefore, my most compelling reason for commending *Good News about Gender* is the profoundly insightful exploration of biblical teachings on gender by examining it using tested exegetical and hermeneutical tools. The Guide is a timely response to address what the author points out should be a major concern to every Christian: 'Misguided interpretations damage the church internally and threaten our witness.' We thoroughly enjoyed reading the book and recommend it as a must-have to all men and women who yearn for an authentic and liberating experience of embodying God's truth."

—Rev. Gideon and Prof. Funmi Para-Mallam (Regional Secretary, International Fellowship of Evangelical Students-English & Portuguese Speaking Africa (IFES-EPSA); National Coordinator, Christian Women for Excellence & Empowerment in Nigerian Society (CWEENS).

GOOD NEWS ABOUT

Gender

A Bible study for young adults

Hannah Rasmussen

Travis + Jen,
May God use this to deepen
your love for his word
and equip many others!
          Hannah Ras-

Christians for Biblical Equality
www.cbeinternational.org

Good News about Gender

Published by Christians for Biblical Equality
122 W Franklin Ave, Suite 218
Minneapolis, MN 55404
www.cbeinternational.org

All Scripture quotations, unless otherwise noted, are taken from THE HOLY BIBLE, NEW INTERNATIONAL VERSION®, NIV® Copyright © 1973, 1978, 1984, 2011 by Biblica, Inc.™ Used by permission. All rights reserved worldwide.

ISBN: 978-1-939971-20-3 (Print)
ISBN: 978-1-939971-21-0 (PDF)
ISBN: 978-1-939971-22-7 (MOBI)
ISBN: 978-1-939971-23-4 (EPUB)

This resource provided in 2016 by **PUBLISH4ALL**
info@publish4all.com

Dedicated to
Ruth Rasmussen,
Mary Horsager,
and
Janice Horsager Rasmussen
2 Timothy 1:5 & Isaiah 51:1–2

Thank you to:

Dad for talking through ideas with me and Mom for shaping the curriculum design.

The rest of my family for being proud of me and cheering me on throughout the process.

Macalester Christian Fellowship & the small group whose late night discussions inspired this topic.

Erin Schulz for co-authoring my first curriculum.

Rick Mattson for developing my leadership through mentoring, trainings, and book recommendations.

Bethel Christian Fellowship and Pastor Jim Olson for teaching me about spiritual gifts and discipleship.

The CRSL chaplains for nurturing me to write about the Bible and gender.

Additional mentors for helping me think through identity and the body.

Christians for Biblical Equality for all your helpful resources and for entrusting me with this project.

Everyone who read over this manuscript for your helpful suggestions, skepticism, and encouragement.

And thank you to God for giving me a reason to wrestle with my questions, for sustaining me through countless revisions, and for shining through this stained glass.

Contents

Why Did I Write This?

I'm a young woman who grew up in the church. I love reading, but I've found that many (non-fiction) Christian books directed specifically at young people focus either on Bible reading, prayer, or dating.

But how does the Word of God speak about how we live in these bodies as young men and women? I'm not asking what the Bible says about marriage or sex or homemaking. I'm talking about who we are, how we relate to each other, what our purpose in life is.

In college, friends from my InterVarsity small group stayed up in my dorm room talking about how we didn't like our culture's blueprints for becoming men and women, but we weren't satisfied with what we found in Christian bookstores either.

How do we care for our own bodies and others'? We decided we had to figure it out together. In our small group, we prayed together for wisdom about what to eat with our mouths, what say with our tongues, what to buy for our bodies to wear. We argued and laughed and cried and apologized. We challenged each other each week to live out what we talked about before we met again.

This experience changed me. I grew in living out my faith in a body—the body of believers, but also my physical body. Inspired by some of our discussions, I decided to write about gender and the church. When I began writing this guide, I was upset with how Christians were distracted from basic faith. As I wrestled with questions about gender and forced myself to continually come back to Scripture, I realized I hadn't been focused on the Bible's main message either. I'd been focusing on the bad news in the world instead of the good news of God. By asking questions and searching for answers in the Bible, I came back to basic truths in a deeper way than before.

In the meantime, I began hearing God call me to a career in ministry. I'd heard different opinions on what the Bible said about women in the church, so I wasn't sure what that could look like for a young woman. I connected with Christians for Biblical Equality through an internship, and began reading more about the topic. God used Scripture, mentors, and the church to confirm my call. Researching for this Bible study has equipped me with biblical reasons for women to use all their God-given gifts. It's also helped me place my own calling in the context of what God's been doing throughout history: using men and women for divine purposes.

My hope is that you too will find a group of friends on the path to becoming men and women of God. My prayer is that you will hear the call to deeper relationships with God and each other. I'm guiding you through my exploration so far, trusting that you'll be able to go further. Together, may we integrate our spiritual lives and our daily lives as women and men, putting flesh on our faith.

Let's live out the good news about gender together.

Before You Begin

Who is this for?

Good News about Gender is designed for:

- **groups:** From organized church classes to people hanging out at someone's house—the size of the group is up to you.
- **of young adults:** Age 18–30, or young adults in spirit!
- **who have questions about the Bible:** Primarily Christians, but could include anyone who has some familiarity with the Bible and is willing to participate in Christian practices.
- **and about gender:** How we connect the Bible and our bodies is a huge topic. We could talk about race, age, sexual orientation, health, gender identity, body image and more. For the purpose of this study, we'll focus on how men and women can integrate their gender into following God.

What will we talk about?

We begin with a foundation in the **Word**. In the introductory session, we build skills for how to understand and apply the Bible.

Unit 1: Identity
First, we discover who we are. We explore what it means for us to be God's adopted children, temples of the Spirit, and a holy priesthood. In each session, we trace a theme through the whole Bible, treating the Bible as one story throughout many times and places.

Unit 2: Community
These two sessions explore our relationships with God and the opposite gender in ministry and marriage. We examine particular chapters of the Bible in depth, paying close attention to the specific history and culture of biblical texts. Then we compare our current time and place and consider what God intended.

Unit 3: Calling
Then we look at how we work together to build up the church body, and what it means to be a disciple of Jesus. For this section, we study the lives of people in the Bible and the function of spiritual gifts.

We close with a focus on the body. We call each other to embody what we've learned as a community, keeping in mind that when this earth fades away, God will give us new bodies.

How will we accomplish this?

Good News about Gender is designed as a guide for group study. I suggest the group choose a host to lead each session. The host could be the same throughout, or different people could lead each session. The group may wish to read through the book aloud together, taking turns reading paragraphs. Or, the host could be more of a teacher, reading the material, drawing the diagrams and leading the activities and discussions. Either way, the host would read through the session before the group meets and make adjustments if necessary. The host will find the activity and resource summary in the back very helpful.

Each session should take about two hours, depending on how long you allow for activities and discussion. Your group may decide to meet each week, every other week, or multiple times a week. Meeting once a week, this study would last for two months. Whatever you decide, I recommend that your group go straight through this book, rather than skipping between this book and another book or resource. This is because each session builds on information from the previous sessions to create one overall story. Each session includes:

❝❞ A theme verse to memorize

 Read: Bible passages (most quotations are from the NIV 2011 if you want to follow along)

 Explore: A group activity

 Watch: A video clip

 Sing: A song to sing together

 Discuss: Questions for discussion with a partner or a small group

 Pray: A prayer to close each session

 Go: A sendoff and call to action

🏆 Challenge: A practical application to complete before the next session

📚 Learn more: Additional books or websites to expand on key concepts

👷 Some sessions give you the chance to **dig deeper.** In the back of the book, you'll find in-depth interpretations of difficult passages for people to read through before that session. I suggest that the host read these to prepare for any questions. If your group is intellectually curious, everyone can read these ahead of time and come prepared for discussion.

Now, shall we begin?

INTRODUCTION

Living Word

" The Word became flesh and made his dwelling among us.**"**
John 1:14

How do we embody or live out God's word as men and women?

That's the question we'll try to answer together throughout *Good News about Gender*. But first we need to know what the word is. We'll devote this whole session to what God's word is and how to understand it.

Words communicate. God "speaks" to people in many ways—through the Bible, prayer, circumstances, and the church community.[1] For now, we'll focus mostly on the Bible. We'll call it "God's word," since it's a unified message God communicates to us. God's word, in whatever form, communicates God's creative and saving power:

- The spoken word of God had the power to create the world (Ps. 33:6, 9).
- The written words of God are more powerful than a double-edged sword (Heb. 4:12).
- Jesus is also the Word of God (Rev. 19:13).

When we seek to deeply know the Bible—God's revelation—we seek to deeply know our God.

The Good Book

The Bible is a collection of letters, historical documents, poems, stories, and prophecies written in the Middle East thousands of years ago. It's a beautifully multifaceted record of God's interaction with his people in history. But it's not always obvious what it means for us today. While God has given us the ability to understand the word, we have to put our skills to use.

When we take God's word seriously, we acknowledge that the Bible comes from a world very different from ours. We also trust that God is still speaking through the text to us today.

Read: Psalm 33, a psalm of praise for God's word.

Psalms were songs written for Israel to sing in praise to God. Psalm 33 instructs people to "sing to him a new song... for the word of the LORD is right and true." To embody this word, either:

Explore and Sing (Option 1)

Write a song praising God for his word. You could break up into groups and give each group five minutes to come up with a short song or poem. Then have a sing-off competition. Or, in a large group, you could each take turns coming up with the next line. Then sing it together! (Host, see the endnote for videos that may give you ideas.)[2]

Explore (Option 2 - for a group with more members or less time):

Using your bodies as letters, try to spell a word from this Psalm! Vote on which group's word was the hardest.

Step 1. What Did the Text Mean Then?

Before we can decide what the text means for us, we need to find out what message the author originally meant to communicate. This process is called **exegesis**, and it includes researching the cultural, historical, and literary context of Scripture.[3]

Even if you've never heard of exegesis, you've probably used it before in its basic form. Imagine that your brother is upset. He hands you his phone and there is a text message from your mom that says, "Your friend is in the hospital. Lol." You might wonder, "Why is she laughing out loud that my brother's friend is in the hospital?"

First, you could look at the **literary context** of the message, reading the messages before and after this text. You could check whether your brother and mom had just been joking or arguing about something. You could ask your brother about the friend. Maybe this friend has a reputation for doing silly stunts or complaining about fake illnesses. Maybe the friend got hurt doing something ridiculous but the injury is minor. You could compare this text to the text messages your mom sends you. Maybe she meant to sign "Mom" but between her and the technology something went wrong and the "L" was recorded instead. Does she often misspell things? Is she usually sarcastic?

If you still don't find a helpful explanation, you might look for **cultural cues**. You could go online and search for "Lol." Some of what you find might be useless—for instance, LOL stands for "League of Legends," an online battle game. Putting that piece of information into the sentence makes no sense at all, so you decide that probably isn't the cultural information your mom intended to communicate.

But then you ask your dad, and you discover that her generation thinks "Lol" means "lots of love," whereas your generation thinks it means "laugh out loud." Suddenly you understand that your mom is the same loving person you always thought she was, and you can explain to your brother that he doesn't need to be upset with her.

Information about the culture, history, or writing style of an author can totally change your interpretation of that person's message. When we try to understand the Bible, information about the culture, history, or writing style of the book's author can help us interpret its message too.

Watch: "Prop Switch" by Studio C (cbe.today/goodnews)

Even in the same cultural or historical context—but with a different prop—a message can have a totally different meaning.

Exegesis: Literary Context

When trying to understand the literary context of a Bible passage, look at things like the tone, structure, and genre of the writing to see what the author is trying to communicate overall.

Sometimes when we read the Bible, we snip out our favorite verses, plaster them on key chains or t-shirts, and immediately act on them. Let's say a student with a poor academic track record decides to apply to medical school. She is sure she will be accepted, because Philippians 4:13 says: "I can do all this through him who gives me strength."

Whether or not she gets into medical school, the student would understand Philippians 4:13 better if she asked a few questions about its literary context.

Let's try this together:

 Read: Philippians 1:1–2, 13, 4:10–19

- What genre is this writing?
- Who is writing to whom?
- Why?
- Where was this written?
- What's the structure of the passage?
- What's the tone?
- What do the surrounding verses tell us about this verse? (See my answers at the bottom of the page)

Philippians is Paul's letter to the church in the town of Philippi to give them advice and encouragement. Paul is in prison for declaring the gospel. Philippians 4:13 is in the first paragraph of a new section about the Philippians' generosity toward Paul. His tone is gratitude and joy. Paul was thanking the Philippians for their generosity, but then felt the need to clarify that he isn't thankful because he was desperate, since God helps him endure. Instead he's thankful that they thought of him and have a long history of generosity in their positive relationship.

When the student considers the literary context of the verse she quotes, she will realize that Paul was not saying God gave him strength to accomplish his own personal goals. He was actually describing how God had not abandoned him when he followed God's call to proclaim the gospel, even though he ended up in prison. God gave him strength to be content in spite of the situation.

To apply the verse, the student might reflect on whether she feels she is following God's call. While this statement does not promise an easy life, she now knows that God will help her be content during hardships—including the difficulty of medical school or the disappointment of not being admitted.

If she wants to imitate Paul, the student could think of people who have supported her in her education and take time to write them a thank you note.

Exegesis: Historical and Cultural Context
Researching a text's historical and cultural context does not mean dismissing its relevance for today. It *does* mean being good stewards of the intellectual material we have access to and doing the work to find out what the text is saying. The Bible has many cultures and histories—and so do we, both as a church and as people in societies. Our perspectives often affect our assumptions when we approach Scripture.

Awareness of our own cultures and the Bible's cultures helps us decipher meaning. For instance, when Jesus says that "the one who has dipped his hand into the bowl with me will betray me" during his last meal with his disciples, people from certain cultures might picture each person sitting at a table with their own bowl and silverware. Was Judas reaching over and grabbing food with his fingers from Jesus' bowl? Someone from another culture might offer a different perspective. In many cultures, people eat with their hands out of a common platter or bowl. An enemy won't poison you if they're eating from the same bowl, so eating together is the ultimate display of trust.

In Jesus' setting, eating together meant something closer to the second idea.[4] Jews became unclean (ritually or spiritually impure) if they ate with Gentiles, but Jesus freely ate with sinners, making a statement that people could enter God's presence without having to first become clean or holy. Jesus shocked the disciples by saying that it wasn't one of those "sinners," but one of his most intimate friends who would betray him—a Jew who he had trusted with his money and his food.

Looking outside our own culture and moment in history opens us up to new ways of understanding God's truth.

The Word became Flesh

 Read: John 1

Literary context: Matthew begins his gospel with a genealogy to show where Jesus came from. In contrast, what new insights does John reveal about where Jesus came from? Notice how John repeats words, almost like poetry. What effect does this have?

Historical and cultural context: The word "word," or *logos* in Greek, had a specific meaning for Greek philosophers at the time. Look up the significance of *logos* using a study Bible, commentary, Bible dictionary, or the internet. How is John using this philosophical concept to speak new ideas to the culture of his day?

According to John, Jesus is the Word in the flesh, a living example of what it meant to love others and honor God. We are also called to embody God's word, living it out with our bodies. "The word of God is alive and active" (Heb. 4:12). Like a play, Scripture is supposed to be alive and acted out, not just sitting on the shelf.[5] That's why exegesis is not enough. We must live out Scripture's teachings in our lives.

Step 2. What Does the Text Mean Today?

The second step in understanding the word is called **hermeneutics**. The way we're using this word, it means figuring out how our interpretations of Scripture have meaning for our lives within our own our contexts.

For example, John 1 introduces readers to Jesus as God mysteriously having become man, bringing light to the world. I heard someone apply this text beautifully to a contemporary context. The setting was a college campus, just before final exams in the middle of a cold and dark winter. For these students craving light and life, the chapel hosted a candlelight service. As the chaplain read John 1, she introduced students to Jesus—the light of the world.

When we listen closely to both our contexts and the Bible, God can speak powerfully into our lives. But we must be careful to distinguish between the two voices. When we proclaim cultural ideals as biblical commands, we give them improper authority.

For example, my mom studied the book of Esther with a group of women. In that book, the king banishes his wife for refusing to display her beauty for his guests. In need of a new wife, the king calls for the most beautiful Persian virgins to come to his palace for a year of beauty treatments. One of them is a Hebrew girl named Esther. She eventually gains the king's favor and uses her position to save the Jewish people from annihilation.

In my mom's group, they interpreted the book of Esther as an encouragement to women to emulate Esther's care for her physical appearance. They suggested that the year of (forced) beauty treatments was the key to her success. I think her dependence on God in fasting and prayer may have had more to do with her ability to influence the king! Advertisements already tell women that being pretty is their most significant accomplishment. This group thought the Bible echoed that narrow message.

The group missed the point. Esther's story is about how God used an orphan girl to save God's people. If Esther could be used by God, anyone could be. If the women had focused on this core truth—trusting God's power—they would have realized that God welcomes them as they are. Unfortunately, the messages women hear about their appearance from society drowned out the voice of the text.

Misguided interpretations damage the church internally and threaten our witness. Instead of advancing the kingdom, we're forced to spend energy healing our church body and building back our credibility with people outside the church. True interpretations embody the word, bringing light and life to the community.

 Discuss:

Are there any specific passages in the Bible that you have struggled to understand? Do you wonder whether certain Bible passages are relevant to today? Explain.

Can you give examples of times when someone thought through the meaning of a text and applied it well to their situation?

The third step is living out the gospel. What is the most beautiful example of living out the gospel you've seen?

3. Show, Don't Tell

All Scripture is God-breathed and is useful for teaching, rebuking, correcting and training in righteousness, so that the servant of God may be thoroughly equipped for every good work. (2 Timothy 3:16–17)

Though Scripture has many uses, its main purpose is to equip us for good work, in other words, for us to live out the message. The final step in interacting with Scripture is **application**.

Christianity is not a religion confined to the lofty spiritual realm. When God became a human as Jesus, God lived out the Word in a body. God chose to honor the physical human body by inhabiting it.[6] God grew inside the body of a young woman. Jesus was born in a body. He experienced growth spurts, hunger, and sleep. When he touched people, miracles happened. His voice and physical presence comforted people. Ultimately, it was his ability to experience pain and even death that brought life to everybody. Jesus was even resurrected back into a body.

Ever since Jesus went back to heaven, the church community worldwide has been Christ's body on earth (Eph. 1:22-23). The Spirit of God dwells among us. We live out the word in our physical bodies. The community (or "body") of Christians show people what the Bible means by our life together. John explains that living out the text matters more than anything else:

> We know that we have come to know him if we keep his commands. Whoever says, "I know him," but does not do what he commands is a liar, and the truth is not in that person. But if anyone obeys his word, love for God is truly made complete in them. This is how we know we are in him: Whoever claims to live in him must live as Jesus did. (1 John 2:5-6)

You may have heard the saying, "People don't read the Bible: they read the Christian." That's not a criticism telling non-Christians to read the Bible more. It is a reminder for Christians that God decided to communicate the gospel through us. As the church, we are Christ's body on earth. How we conduct our internal and external affairs does not merely affect our testimony. How we act is itself our testimony, our witness to the world of the power of the living God.

 Discuss:

Does exegesis, hermeneutics, or application come most naturally to you? Which is hardest?

When have you seen people skip one of these steps? How did it affect 1) the message? 2) the Christian community? 3) people outside the community?

 Pray:

God, thank you for revealing your Word to us in the person of Jesus and in the Bible. We trust that you are alive and active among us. Speak to us throughout these sessions so that we may know you better. We ask for the strength to seek you diligently and the courage to live out what we find.

The Word Embodied

Throughout this guide, we will spend a lot of time looking at what the Bible has to say. We'll look at two levels: close up and far away. When trying to put a puzzle together, it's useful to see the big photo on the box to know how the little pieces fit together, but it's also useful to see two pieces next to each other and compare the edges and the colors on each one. In order to figure out God's message, we'll study individual verses and interpret them in their literary, historical, and cultural contexts (exegesis and hermeneutics). We'll also do what's called biblical theology—looking at the Bible as a unified story of God's relationship with people across time and place. We'll focus on themes in order to understand how parts of God's message fit together into one big picture.

Then, we want to think carefully about how the text applies to us, two millennia or more after these events happened. After the Bible study sections of each session, we'll discover basic principles from the lesson and discuss how they apply to our lives. Once we know this, we get to our final goal—living it out. We'll challenge each other to apply the text before the coming session.

 Challenge: Memorize the theme verse

In order to embody God's word, we first need to embed it in our minds. Each session in this guide begins with a theme verse for the group to memorize before the next session. You may want to create a song, dance, or piece of artwork that will help you remember it. For this session, our verse is John 1:14. (If you'd like an extra challenge, you can memorize all of John 1.) Come back next time ready to recite the memory verse and share what you learned about God's living word.

 Go:

Until we meet again, let us seek to understand and live out God's word in our community.

 Learn more:

How to Read the Bible for All Its Worth by Gordon D. Fee and Douglas Stuart
This handbook gives an easy-to-understand but thorough explanation of what exegesis and hermeneutics are. The authors give helpful tips for interpreting each major genre of the Bible—from letters to prophecy, wisdom literature to Old Testament narratives.

The Blue Parakeet: Rethinking How You Read the Bible by Scot McKnight
In this book, Scot McKnight challenges us not to treat the Bible like a parakeet, clipping its wings to tame it and keep it in a cage. Everyone picks and chooses how to apply the Bible to their lives, but how should we decide which parts to apply? He uses the example of passages about women in the church to show how people interpret and apply Scripture differently.

UNIT 1
Our Identity

We are God's children, and God has given us all things—most of all the Spirit's presence. God lives in us and in the community of the church.

To discover this, we'll take a panoramic view of the whole biblical landscape. We'll trace a single theme through the entire story of the Bible, noticing the direction God has been moving throughout history.

Adopted Children with an Inheritance

> **❝** There is neither Jew nor Gentile, neither slave nor free, nor is there male and female, for you are all one in Christ Jesus. If you belong to Christ, then you are Abraham's seed, and heirs according to the promise. **❞**
> Galatians 3:28-29

 Challenge Check-in:

Can you say last session's theme verse?

What did you learn about God's living word?

 Explore:

Ask someone to read the following script while the rest of the group demonstrates it visually. Use a Monopoly board to represent plots of land and toy figurines to represent people. If your group doesn't have Monopoly, they could draw illustrations on a large piece of paper or act out the situation with random props.

[Set up the Monopoly board with houses or hotels but give one "king" figurine all the Monopoly deeds.]

Imagine writing the laws for a country where everyone farms, but land is limited. These people have just gained independence from a king who owned all the land and made the people work it for him. The new government announces a shockingly democratic decision—they will divide the land between the existing families of citizens.

[The Monopoly deeds are now available for sale. Organize figurines into families. Give each family all the matching deeds of a color or two.]

Men will represent their families. Since virtually everyone marries and has children, sons will inherit their father's land. Daughters will participate in their husband's inheritance.

[Show a woman marrying and moving to her husband's plot.]

To keep the land in the family, each family needs to produce an heir, a son. However, if the father has many sons and not much land, it's possible that the sons would not have enough land to support their families. The little farms might have to be sold to other families. Then some families would grow rich at the expense of others.

[Show a family losing money as they travel around the board, having to sell a property.]

To prevent misfortune from becoming a cycle of generational poverty, no family can permanently buy land from another. They can lease land, but everything goes back to the original family owners on the seventieth year. This will also limit the risk of foreign investors buying up land and using their financial power to influence governance.

[Redistribute the deeds.]

But to keep the family from having to sell their land in the first place, every father will give his firstborn son twice as much land as his brothers. If the harvest is poor, some family members may have to sell their land. But since one brother has a larger plot, he is more likely to be able to at least keep his part of the land in the family. The eldest brother is also expected to act as a father to the other siblings, providing for them or buying land from his brothers in a financial crisis.

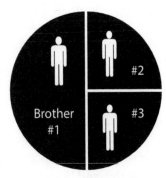

[Demonstrate the eldest brother's double plot, and how he can prevent one of the plots of the family's color from being sold out of the family.]

If there are no sons in the family, a daughter may inherit. If she does, she must marry someone from her clan. This way, her family's land doesn't end up as part of another clan's inheritance and create power imbalances between clans.

[Demonstrate the only child daughter marrying someone of a neighboring plot to keep her family's land together.]¹

The people of Israel had just come out of slavery in Egypt. God promised them the land of Canaan, told them how to divide it up and gave them the laws we just described.² God's law provided all people with land, which meant crops, which meant life.

The Sign of Belonging

Centuries before, this nation had been "one man, and he as good as dead" (Heb. 11:12). God promised to give Abraham the land of Canaan and make him "the father of many nations." But he was not a father at all. No matter how much God blessed Abraham, if he had no heir, the blessing would stop with him.

📖 Read: Genesis 15, 17

Literary context: Abraham and God interacted using the vocabulary and style of a legal contract. God and Abraham made a covenant.

Cultural context: The blood of animals often sealed a formal contract (15:9-11, 17-18).³

What did God promise Abraham the first time? What did Abraham have to do?

What did God offer Abraham the second time? How did Abraham seal the covenant? (See my answers at the bottom of the next page.)

In response to God's promise, each man in Abraham's household had his foreskin cut off. This was to remind him that if he did not follow God faithfully, he would be cut off from the people (17:14).[4] As promised, God provided a son for Abraham. The descendants of Abraham became the nation of Israel, who settled in the land of Canaan. From the time of Abraham on, all men in this community have been circumcised as a sign that they belong to a people who have a covenant with God.

The People of God

To determine not only *who* belonged, but *how* they belonged to the community, Israelites kept records of their family lineage through genealogies. Among other things, these lists of names helped settle land disputes and allocate inheritance.[5]

The genealogy of Jesus certifies him as a Jewish freeman. It explains how he belongs to the covenant people of Abraham and inherits the kingship of David. He therefore fulfills the qualifications of the Messiah or "anointed one"—the ultimate prophet / king / priest God promised to send to deliver Israel. But it also tells where Jesus comes from. Who was Jesus' family?

 Explore:

Choose someone to act as a game show host, an employer in a job interview, or a judge in a courtroom. Choose another person to be a detective. Assign each of the following characters to other people in the room and give each person five minutes to look up Bible stories about their character:

- Abraham (Gen. 12:10–20)
- Jacob (Gen. 27:5–36)
- Judah and Tamar (Gen. 38)
- Rahab (Josh. 2)

God promised Abraham a reward the first time—an heir and land. Abraham's side of the deal was to believe and confirm the covenant by cutting animals. The second time, God reassured Abraham that he would receive God's loyal protection (17:8), land (17:8), and a son as an heir (17:16). Abraham had to seal this covenant by cutting human skin. His part of the covenant was to practice a constant reminder of this agreement by circumcising all males in his household for generations to come (17:12).

- Ruth (Ruth 1:1-5, 4:9-22)
- David and Uriah's wife Bathsheba (2 Sam. 11)
- Solomon (1 Kings 11:13)
- Mary (Matt. 1:18-25)

Then have the interviewer question each person to determine their character's social and religious standing, asking things like:

Are you the firstborn? An Israelite? A man? What is your reputation?

Have you broken God's covenant?

What dark secrets do you have in your past?

When the interviewer pronounces that none of these people are fit to be in Jesus' family, ask the detective to suddenly discover a legal document and read out Matthew 1:1-16.

You would expect God's Son incarnate—Jesus—to have ancestors who were flawless heroes. Instead, Jesus' earthly lineage includes youngest sons, women, and Gentiles (foreigners). It includes a widow, a pregnant teen, a murderer, a cheat, a liar, a mistress, a womanizer, a prostitute and a solicitor of prostitutes. Yet by grace, God considered these people worthy to be part of Jesus' lineage.

But God chose the foolish things of this world to shame the wise; God chose the weak things of the world to shame the strong. God chose the lowly things of this world and the despised things—and the things that are not—to nullify the things that are, so that no one may boast before him. (1 Corinthians 1:27-29)

Paul explains that God highlights his abundant favor by giving it to people that society views as undeserving. Then it is clear that God's power, not the person's social status or religious observance, is the cause.

[H]e said to me, 'My grace is sufficient for you, for my power is made perfect in weakness.' ...When I am weak, then I am strong. (2 Cor. 12:9-10)

 Discuss:

When has God used you (or someone you know) in spite of a particular weakness to display divine grace?

The Son's Inheritance

Jesus was a free Jewish man and a popular teacher, but he didn't seek prestige and influence. Other famous ancient teachers avoided associating themselves too much with those viewed as weak. Gordon Fee uses Socrates as an example:

> [A]ccording to Diogenes Laertius, Socrates used to say every day that 'there are three blessings for which he was grateful to Fortune: first, that I was born a human being, and not one of the brutes; next that I was born a man and not a woman; thirdly, a Greek and not a barbarian.' This obviously influenced the famous rabbinical prayer "Blessed are you, O God, ... that I'm not a brute creature, nor a Gentile, nor a woman."[6]

Socrates' phrase reflected how women were viewed for four hundred years until Jesus' time. The fact that Jewish rabbis, who gained influence after Jesus' time, prayed something similar shows that Jesus came into a culture where being a woman was considered almost a curse.

But Jesus stepped into this context to teach a different philosophy. Jesus didn't thank God for his special status. Rather, he humbled himself (Phil. 2) and went out of his way to associate with those whom society had rejected.

He was the "firstborn of all creation" (Col. 1:15) appointed by God as "the heir of all things" (Heb. 1:2). As the only person capable of fulfilling the law, Jesus deserved all the blessings promised to those who obeyed the law, as well as the inheritance the law promised Israelite men. But he didn't champion the law to protect his own benefits. Rather, Jesus freed us from law. He began a new system based on God's grace. God's firstborn son, Jesus, inherited all things. Since he died, his inheritance could be divided up again. So our heavenly Father gave us this inheritance! Paul says:

He who did not spare his own Son, but gave him up for us all—how will he not also, along with him, graciously give us all things? (Romans 8:32)

All things are yours, whether Paul or Apollos or Cephas or the world or life or death or the present or the future—all are yours, and you are of Christ, and Christ is of God. (1 Corinthians 3:21b–22)

In Israelite law, only sons inherited. But now, all Christian men and women have access to our spiritual inheritance as "sons" of God.

Therefore you are no longer a slave, but a son; and if a son, then an heir through God. (Galatians 4:7, NASB)

We don't have to earn membership into the community through inward or outward signs of obedience. We are simply "reborn" into the family. Jesus' death was the ultimate act of humility. He gave up his status and allowed the rest of God's children to inherit all things! While Socrates taught a hierarchy, Jesus brings mutuality and shared authority:

There is neither Jew nor Gentile, neither slave nor free, nor is there male and female, for you are all one in Christ Jesus. If you belong to Christ, then you are Abraham's seed, and heirs according to the promise. (Galatians 3:28–29)

 Discuss:

Deep down, what unwritten rules do you feel like God requires for someone to be part of his people?

The Church as God's People
As the gospel spread across the Roman Empire, Jesus' followers had to rethink who was included in Christ's new covenant community and what the requirements were for membership. God had given Israel laws to govern a nation, its customs, and its economy. But God's new people were not confined within national borders nor were they playing similar parts in their various economic systems. The new community was the church.

Paul argued that the Gentiles should be members of the church community. Since circumcision separated Jews and Gentiles, Paul strategically focused on Abraham, the father of Judaism and the first person to be circumcised. Paul explains that, in fact, circumcision wasn't the point:

> Circumcision was a sign that Abraham already had faith and that God had already accepted him and declared him to be righteous— even before he was circumcised. So Abraham is the spiritual father of those who have faith but have not been circumcised. They are counted as righteous because of their faith. And Abraham is also the spiritual father of those who have been circumcised, but only if they have the same kind of faith Abraham had before he was circumcised. (Romans 4:11–12, NLT)

Paul points out that Abraham was considered righteous for his faith (as we read in Gen. 15) before the covenant was reaffirmed and sealed with circumcision (Gen. 17). This makes Abraham the father of everyone who acts on their faith, regardless of their circumcision status.[7]

The Holy Spirit and Baptism as Sign of Belonging
Instead of circumcision, God gave the new community new signs to mark that they belonged to God's people. God gave the Holy Spirit and the symbol of baptism, opening the door for men and women, Jew and Gentile, to be part of the church community. Peter discovered this when God asked him to preach to God-fearing Gentiles:

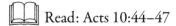 Read: Acts 10:44–47

The Holy Spirit had descended at Jesus' baptism and on Pentecost. When the Spirit entered the Gentiles, Peter realized God was including the Gentiles in the new community of Jesus-followers. In those days, anyone who followed a rabbi (religious teacher) would be baptized to symbolize their allegiance to the teacher. Peter realized the Gentiles, too, had been accepted by Jesus as his followers. They, too, were able to show their commitment to following Jesus through the outward sign of water baptism.

When the leaders of the early church heard Peter's story (Acts 11:18) and how the Holy Spirit was working among the Gentiles (Acts 15:1–35), they decided that circumcision no longer determined who was part of God's people. Now, what identifies us as belonging to God's community is the Holy Spirit:

> The Spirit himself testifies with our spirit that we are God's children. Now if we are children, then we are heirs—heirs of God and co-heirs with Christ, if indeed we share in his sufferings in order that we may also share in his glory. (Romans 8:16–17)

We will inherit everything Christ inherits—both suffering and glory. The Holy Spirit is the first installment of our inheritance, which guarantees everything God has promised us (2 Cor. 1:22).

 Discuss:

What's your relationship like with the Holy Spirit?

Forming Perfect Union
With circumcision, only men could participate in this symbol of inclusion in God's covenant people. With the Holy Spirit as the new sign of God's people, now the uncircumcised, like Gentiles and women, can have full access to "the incomparable riches of his grace" (see Eph. 2:6-13). They too can be baptized into the new covenant community. Under grace, now anyone adopted into God's family has the son's rights of inheritance.

While the people of Israel inherited a plot of land in tiny Canaan, God's people in the church inherit a new spacious Promised Land—a new heaven and a new earth. While each male Israelite inherited land for their family in order to maintain equality between family groupings, in Christ's community all believers are incorporated into God's family. We are one tribe with Jesus as our head. Differences in status don't define us.

There is nothing about your gender, ethnicity, religious upbringing, social status, nationality, or race that can keep God from choosing and using you. After all, God gave us our bodies too. When choosing who will lead his people, "the LORD does not look at the things people look at. People look at the outward appearance, but the LORD looks at the heart." (1 Sam. 16:7).

In addition, just like Jesus' ancestors, you're never too broken to fulfill mighty purposes. The Holy Spirit inside you will shine through your cracks. Thank God that when we are at our weakest, God's grace is brightest.

 Watch:

"I Know Who I Am" by Sinach
(cbe.today/goodnews)

Gospel artist Sinach celebrates our identity in Christ with a church in her native Nigeria.

 Pray:

Father, sometimes we feel we need to earn your approval or that we're not qualified to be part of your family. But you adopted us with unconditional love! You deposit your Spirit in us to guarantee our inheritance. Thank you for assuring us that we are your children. We are so glad to belong in your family.

 Sing:

"Be Thou My Vision"
Lyrics by Dallan Forgaill in the 8th century
Translated from ancient Irish by Mary E. Byrne, 1905
Versified by Eleanor H. Hull, 1912
(cbe.today/goodnews)

Be Thou my Vision, O Lord of my heart;
Naught be all else to me, save that Thou art.
Thou my best Thought, by day or by night,
Waking or sleeping, Thy presence my light.

Be Thou my Wisdom, and Thou my true Word;
I ever with Thee and Thou with me, Lord;

Thou my great Father, I Thy true son;
Thou in me dwelling, and I with Thee one.

Be Thou my battle Shield, Sword for the fight;
Be Thou my Dignity, Thou my Delight;
Thou my soul's Shelter, Thou my high Tower:
Raise Thou me heavenward, O Power of my power.

Riches I heed not, nor man's empty praise,
Thou mine Inheritance, now and always:
Thou and Thou only, first in my heart,
High King of Heaven, my Treasure Thou art.

High King of Heaven, my victory won,
May I reach Heaven's joys, O bright Heaven's Sun!
Heart of my own heart, whatever befall,
Still be my Vision, O Ruler of all.

 Challenge: Learn about the global church

Once again, we'll memorize this session's theme verse together. Also, we'll each talk to someone from another country about their home church before the next session. You could talk to someone who immigrated to your country, contact a missionary, or connect with a local church in another country. Ask them: what does it mean to you to be part of the global church body? What is God doing in your community? How can we pray for you? Come back ready to share about God's people around the world.

 Go:

Until we meet again, let us cross barriers to unite as family under Jesus' name.

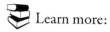 Learn more:

Christians for Biblical Equality www.cbeinternational.org
This organization believes that the Bible, properly interpreted, teaches the fundamental equality of men and women of all ethnic groups, all

economic classes, and all age groups, based on the teachings of Scriptures such as Galatians 3:28. Their website contains free articles, book recommendations, and a blog on gender related issues. They also publish journals and booklets like the one you are reading.

Kingdom without Borders: The Untold Story of Global Christianity by Miriam Adeney.
Christianity may be losing popularity in the West, but it is growing rapidly in the global South. Adeney tells stories of everyday believers as well as renowned church leaders throughout the world. She beautifully describes what God is doing in and through the church, inviting us to celebrate how each region contributes something new to our understanding of God.

Priests and God's Temple

" Don't you know that you yourselves are God's temple and that God's Spirit dwells in your midst? ...you together are that temple. **"**
1 Corinthians 3:16–17

 Challenge Check-in:

Can you say last session's theme verse?

What did you find out about the global church?

 Explore:

Choose either these groups of photos:
"The World's 50 Most Unusual Churches" or
"17 Awe-Inspiring Places Of Worship Around The World"
(cbe.today/goodnews)

Show the group these photos either on a screen or printed out. What does the physical appearance of each place make you feel?

Ask everyone to pick one they find most interesting. What does the architecture say about the community that worships there and who they worship?

The Tabernacle
In this session, we're going to tell the story of how God has lived among people throughout history.

God has always been with the chosen people. When the Israelites fled Egypt, "by day the LORD went ahead of them in a pillar of cloud to guide them on their way and by night in a pillar of fire to give them light" (Ex. 13:21). Shortly after the LORD gave Moses the Ten Commandments and several other laws, the LORD asked Moses to go back up Mount Sinai. Moses received seven more chapters of instructions, this time explaining how to build and furnish the tabernacle and what priests' duties were. If Moses followed the blueprint exactly, God promised:

> I will consecrate the tent of meeting and the altar and will consecrate Aaron and his sons to serve me as priests. Then I will dwell among the Israelites and be their God. They will know that I am the LORD their God, who brought them out of Egypt so that I might dwell among them. I am the LORD their God. (Exodus 29:44–46)

God lived among the Israelites in a tent, traveling with them through the desert until they reached the Promised Land. The LORD wanted them to know who their God was.

God wanted to be at the center of Israelite society—its geography, law, economics, and social life. When the Israelites set up camp, the tabernacle went in the middle and everyone else arranged themselves around it (Num. 2:2). The Israelites kept their law on stone tablets in the tabernacle, settled debts with sacrifices at the tabernacle, and gathered for festivals at the tabernacle.

The Priests

The tabernacle was run by priests. God also gave specific instructions about priestly qualifications and duties. Only men from the tribe of Levi were priests. It was a full time, life-long job. Unlike the rest of Israel, they didn't farm. They gave God offerings of worship and performed sacrifices for forgiveness. The leftovers from sacrifices were their food. They were set apart for God, or "holy."

Only priests could enter the tabernacle. Only the high priest could enter the Holy of Holies, only once a year, to offer sacrifices for the whole country's sin that year (Lev. 16:2–3, 34, Heb. 9:7). According to Jewish tradition, the high priest walked in with a rope around his waist or ankle. If he fell dead, they could pull his body out! These boundaries reminded the people that the God who lived among them was still separate from them. God was holy.

 Discuss:

God is holy but also lives among us. What does this mean for your relationship with God?

The Temple

When the Israelites reached Canaan, they conquered the land bit by bit. God eventually appointed a king and secured its borders (1 Kings 5:4–5). Soon the Israelites were no longer wandering nomads. They were a kingdom. King David established Jerusalem as Israel's capitol and built himself a beautiful palace. From there, he ruled the country. But he realized God was the real ruler of the country, and felt ashamed that God's "house" was a tent (2 Sam. 7:1–2). He wanted to build God a beautiful palace too—a temple.

Under the direction of God's Spirit, King David drew up building plans for the temple. But God chose David's son, King Solomon, to carry them out (1 Chron. 28:6, 11–12). King Solomon used the most expensive building materials. Anyone who visited this temple would know that Israel's God was worthy of beauty and expense. Then the rest of the world would worship God.

Read: 1 Kings 10:4-9

A woman who ruled a foreign kingdom acknowledged that Israel's God reigned over the world. What a witness to God's power!

But King Solomon began to worship the gods of his foreign wives. He set up shrines to these gods, rather than worshipping God in his temple in

Herod's Temple
on the Temple Mount

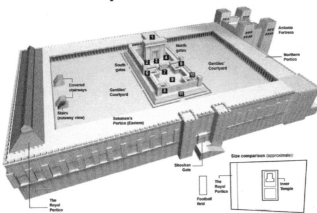

1. Holy Place
2. Altar
3. Priests' Courtyard
4. Israelites' Courtyard
5. Chamber of Lepters
6. Chamber of Oils
7. Gate of Nicanor
8. Chamber of Nazarites
9. Womens' Courtyard
10. Chamber of Wood
11. The Gate Beautiful

Image Copyright Faithlife
Corporation, makers of
Logos Bible Software –
www.logos.com

Jerusalem. Because Solomon stopped making God the center of his life and God's temple the center of the nation, God split Israel into two kingdoms.

Eventually, Solomon's temple was defiled and then destroyed by the Babylonians. The Babylonians captured many Jews and took them into exile. The people were torn from each other and their homeland. How could God dwell among them now?

Set Apart

Later, some exiles returned from Babylon. They rebuilt the temple in Jerusalem, although it was less impressive than Solomon's temple (Ezra 3:12, 6:13). By Jesus' time, Herod the Great had built a new temple on top of it.[1] Like in the tabernacle, different people were allowed access to different parts of the building. God-fearing Gentiles were allowed only in the outer court. Jewish women could enter the next area, but Jewish men could go one level further. The rest was reserved for priests.

A sign used to be on the balustrade (temple fence). It says, in Greek: "Foreigners must not enter inside the balustrade or into the forecourt around the sanctuary. Whoever is caught will have himself to blame for his ensuing death."

Jesus as Temple and High Priest

God is holy and set apart, but also wants to be close to people. So God became human and took the name Jesus. Jesus was also called "Emmanuel"—God with us.

Jesus revolutionized the boundaries between God and people. Jesus was mysteriously both God and human. His body was like a temple—where God and people meet. He told the Pharisees they could destroy this temple and he would raise it in three days (John 2:19–22). They didn't understand he was talking about raising himself from the dead.

 Read: Hebrews 9:11–15, 10:19–22

Jesus was also a priest. He never sinned. He was holy. He brought a sacrifice to God for the people's sin—himself. At the moment that Jesus died, the curtain to the Holy of Holies in Herod's temple was torn from top to bottom (Matt. 27:50–52). No human could reach high enough to tear the curtain. Through Jesus, God had reached down and removed the barrier between humanity and holiness.

🎵 Sing:

"Jesus at the Center of it All"
by Israel Houghton, 2012 (decade version)
(cbe.today/goodnews)

Jesus be the center of my life
Jesus be the center of my life
From beginning to the end
It'll always be, it's always been you Jesus, Jesus

Chorus:
Nothing else matters
Nothing in this world will do
Jesus be the center
Everything revolves around you, only you

Jesus at the center of it all
Jesus at the center of it all
From beginning to the end
It'll always be, it's always been you Jesus, Jesus

Chorus

Bridge:
From my heart to the heavens,
Jesus be the center
It's all about you
Yes, it's all about you

Bridge

Jesus be the center of your church
Jesus be the center of your church
From beginning to the end
It'll always be, it's always been you Jesus, Jesus

God's Spirit with Us

After Jesus rose from the dead, he returned to heaven. Just before he left, he told his followers, "Surely I am with you always" (Matt. 28:20). He told them to wait in Jerusalem. Soon they would see a new way of God living with people.

The apostles, the women who followed Jesus, and Jesus' birth family waited and prayed in Jerusalem (Acts 1:12–14). The apostles (and possibly the rest of this group) were together to celebrate Pentecost, or the Feast of Weeks. On this Jewish festival, the people met to "rejoice at the place the Lord will choose for the dwelling of his name" (Deut. 16:9–2).[2] But at this Pentecost, the Holy Spirit revealed that God would dwell in a new place.

> Suddenly a sound like the blowing of a violent wind came from heaven and filled the whole house where they were sitting. They saw what seemed to be tongues of fire that separated and came to rest on each of them. All of them were filled with the Holy Spirit and began to speak in other tongues as the Spirit enabled them. (Acts 2:2–4)

The fire and the wind were the first symbols of God's presence with the Israelites over 1000 years earlier. God's visible Spirit was back!

God's New Temple

But God did not appear in the temple. In fact, that temple was destroyed by the Romans in AD 70 and has never been rebuilt. For the first time, God chose to live in and among God's followers themselves.

God-fearing foreigners had come to worship at Herod's temple for the Pentecostal festival. They would stay on the edge and worship outside the fence. But they heard the commotion and gathered around Jesus' followers. Here was God's Spirit speaking directly to them in their own languages! God seemed to be saying that these foreigners were welcome, that anyone could speak directly to God without going to a priest or needing translation into Hebrew. Paul later explained that they too were part of the new dwelling God was building:

> Don't you know that you yourselves are God's temple and that God's Spirit dwells in your midst?...you together are that temple. (1 Corinthians 3:16–17)

> Consequently, you are no longer foreigners and strangers, but fellow citizens with God's people and also members of his household, built on the foundation of the apostles and prophets, with Christ Jesus himself as the chief cornerstone. In him the whole building is joined together and rises to become a holy temple in the Lord. And in him you too are being built together to become a dwelling in which God lives by his Spirit. (Ephesians 2:19–22)

God's New Priests

When Peter saw the Spirit speaking through ordinary believers at Pentecost, he realized this was the fulfillment of Jesus' promise and an earlier prophecy. He announced to the crowd of onlookers:

Read: Acts 2:16–18

A new era had begun. Every believer would be a priest or a prophet, regardless of gender, age, or ethnicity. Peter explained this idea further in a letter to church members:

Read: 1 Peter 2:4-5, 9

 Discuss:

List aloud the phrases describing God's people in this passage. What do these mean in the historical context we talked about earlier? Compare this to Exodus 19:5-6. Who is God talking to? Who is God talking about?

When people saw the beauty of God's previous dwellings and the justice of the community of the chosen people, they worshipped God. We are also chosen "that [we] may declare the praises" of God. How do you and your church community reflect God's beauty, justice and forgiveness to bring praise to God?

 Watch:

"Holy Week Women" by Hannah Rasmussen (cbe.today/goodnews)

Even before God poured out the Spirit on both men and women at Pentecost, biblical women played an important role in God's salvation story. This spoken word highlights their often forgotten stories. How might God use you to proclaim the good news?

A Spirit-Centered People
The Spirit's presence changed the community of believers.

 Read: Acts 2:42–47

In summary: In Acts, the church centered every part of life around God. They celebrated together. Their politics transcended ethnic boundaries. Their economy was based on generosity, sharing all they had with each other and the poor. Their geography was directed by God—go to all the earth.

The Spirit's new dwelling is in the community of the church. The church displays God's beauty, showing the world God is worth worshipping. The church is the place we find forgiveness. The church is where God meets people and speaks our language.

Pray:

Spirit, thank you for dwelling inside us and among the church community. Give us confidence to approach you directly as your priests. Fill us with words to speak as your prophets. As we center our lives around you, may our community display your beauty and justice to the watching world.

 Challenge: Silent retreat

Before the next session, spend some time alone in silence. If you've never done something like this before, start with one hour. If this isn't your first time, stretch yourself a little further than before.

Bring your Bible and a journal to a calm environment. If you want, take Christian music or art supplies. Whatever you do, focus on praying and listening for the Spirit's voice.

For part of that time, imagine that your heart or soul is a house. Perhaps the living room represents your relationships, the closet represents your fears, and so forth. Imagine giving a tour. How do you feel about showing the Holy Spirit around? Which parts of the house have you invited the Holy Spirit into?[3]

Come back to the group ready to share what you learned about how it feels to be God's temple.

 Go:

Until we meet again, let us make the Spirit feel at home in our bodies and our community.

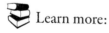 Learn more:

Jesus Have I Loved, but Paul?: A Narrative Approach to the Problem of Pauline Christianity by J. R. Daniel Kirk
After reading the stories of Jesus' life, Paul's letters can seem theological,

complicated, and even offensive. But, if we look at both the Gospels and Paul's writings as part of one big story about the people of God, we begin to see Paul in a new light. J. R. Kirk's book looks at the stories Paul invites people into—stories about God including the marginalized and working through the church to redeem creation. (Want to see a trailer? Visit cbe.today/goodnews)

Women Called to Witness: Evangelical Feminism in the 19th Century by Nancy A. Hardesty.
In 19th century America, the women's movement advocated for temperance, voting rights, and the abolition of slavery. Hardesty explains that this social change was inspired and implemented by evangelical Christians. Christ's central place in these activists' lives enabled them to reform marriage, politics and society.

UNIT 2
Our Community

Men and women accomplish God's mission by working together. God's love empowers us to serve each other in church, marriages and the community.

To discover this, we'll zoom in to short passages. We'll study a chapter or so in depth, discovering its historical, cultural, and literary contexts. We'll also look at our own cultural contexts.

Created Allies

❝ One of the teachers of the law [asked Jesus], "Of all of the commandments, which is the most important?" "The most important one," answered Jesus, "is this: 'Hear, O Israel: The Lord our God, the Lord is one. Love the Lord your God with all your heart and with all your soul and with all your mind and with all your strength. The second is this: 'Love your neighbor as yourself.' There is no commandment greater than these. ❞
Mark 12:28–31

 Challenge Check-in:

Can you say last session's theme verse?

How was your silent retreat?

 Explore:

Quickly list on a blackboard / whiteboard or a large sheet of paper: what top five things does your culture associate with being "manly" or "masculine"? What about "feminine," "ladylike" or "girly"?

Create a new list, this time listing characteristics of the God the Father, Jesus or the Holy Spirit (inclubnding the fruits of the Holy Spirit). Circle the characteristics of God that humans can reflect.

Now compare this with the first two lists. What overlaps do you see?

What gaps do you notice?

Made in the Image of the Trinity

> So God created human beings in his own image. In the image of God he created them; male and female he created them. (Genesis 1:27, NLT)[1]

We can't mirror all of God's qualities (for instance, his almighty power), but humans do have the unique privilege of bearing God's image. For example: like God, humans can create beauty and order. We can think abstract thoughts and feel empathy.[2]

A Celtic symbol for the Trinity, made from overlapping fish symbols

 Discuss:

How do the statements below make you feel?

- You don't have to act a certain way to "be a man" or justify your femininity. Your gender is inherently part of your being as a man or woman created by God.
- You don't have to perform to be a man or woman "of God." You already belong to God.
- If we can't ever pinpoint how each gender reflects God's image differently, that won't diminish the Creator's beautiful, mysterious design.

Then God blessed them and said, "Be fruitful and multiply. Fill the earth and govern it. Reign over the fish in the sea, the birds in the sky, and all the animals that scurry along the ground." (Genesis 1:28, NLT)

Humans also resemble the Trinity in their God-given responsibility to steward the earth by working together. The love among the Father, Son, and Holy Spirit empowers the persons of the Trinity to work together to bring glory to God and rule creation (see Matt. 3:16–17). In the same way, loving God and each other enables us to care for creation.

Allies

 Read: Genesis 2:15–25

Cultural and literary context: God gave Adam an ally for the task of caring for Eden. Some translations call Eve a "helpmeet" or "suitable helper." The Hebrew phrase is *ezer kenegdo*. *Kenegdo* means corresponding, equal and opposite. Twice in the Bible the word *ezer* refers to a woman. But it refers to God sixteen times—all in a military context. God is Israel's ally—a powerful defender against threats, and an equal partner in mission. Eve was created in God's image—the image of an *ezer*. She was Adam's equal and powerful ally in carrying out God's purposes.[3]

Although it wasn't exactly a trinity of equal members (God being far superior to humans), this alliance of God, man, and woman was a powerful trio.

> Though one may be overpowered, two can defend themselves. A cord of three strands is not quickly broken. (Ecclesiastes 4:12)

Together, Adam and Eve could carry out all God's commands—caring for the Creator by caring for all creation. They could bring forth life in abundance from the ground and from their union. The two most important commands would hold this team together: loving God and loving each other.

> One of the teachers of the law [asked Jesus], "Of all of the commandments, which is the most important?" "The most important one," answered Jesus, "is this: 'Hear, O Israel: The Lord our God, the Lord is one. Love the Lord your God with all your heart and with all your soul and with all your mind and with all your strength. The second is this: 'Love your neighbor as yourself.' There is no commandment greater than these." (Mark 12:28–31)

The Broken Alliance

So the evil one decided to divide and conquer. His strategy was to attack the relationships between people and God and between man and woman.

 Read: Genesis 3:1–24

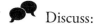 Discuss:

What doubts and desires did the serpent stir up in the woman?

Where was the man when the woman was tempted?

When God confronted them, who did each of them blame? (Check your answers at the bottom of the page.)

The woman and man believed the lie that they needed something more to become like God. They both forgot that they were already made in God's image. When they blamed God, each other and creation, they reflected the image of the Accuser—which is Satan's name in Hebrew.[4]

God explained that sin and blame had now distorted their relationships. Adam, whose life came out of dust, would painfully labor to produce a livelihood out of the earth from then on. Eve, whose life came from Adam, would now struggle in her relationship with him. He would domineer over her. And, she too would experience painful labor to produce life through childbirth.

When Adam and Eve ate fruit from the Tree of the Knowledge of Good and Evil, they got what they wanted in a twisted sense. Rather than the discernment between good and evil, they now "knew" evil from experience—by receiving the terrible consequences of their sin. Disobeying God's command made it harder to fulfill God's original instruction to subdue the earth, be fruitful, and multiply.

Saving Trios

Even though Adam and Eve tried to break the alliance between God and people, God never gave up on using men and women to care for creation. I'm not just referring to married couples. God works through married and single people, men and women who are friends, siblings, cousins, parent and child, coworkers, and even distant relatives in-law. In fact, men and

---

The serpent made the woman doubt God's instructions and God's character. It told her that she was not yet like God, but by eating from the tree she could know good and evil like God. The man was with the woman (v.6). When God confronted the man, the man blamed both the woman and God, saying "the woman you gave me" was responsible. She in turn blamed the serpent.

women worked together to save God's people at every critical juncture in biblical history. God used:

- Miriam, Moses, and Aaron to save Israel from slavery in Egypt (Ex. 2:1–10, 4:13–16, 4:27–5:1, 15:20–21, 28:1)
- Barak, Deborah,and Jael to save Israel from Canaanite oppressors (Judg. 4–5)
- Ruth and Boaz to save Naomi's family line so that King David would be be born (Ruth 2:1–4:17)
- Hannah, Eli, and Samuel to save Israel from spiritual ruin (1 Sam. 1)
- Esther and Mordecai to save the Jews in Persia from genocide (Est. 3:13–5:2)
- Jesus' disciples and the women who followed him to support and continue Jesus' saving work (Luke 8:1–3, John 20:1–18, Acts 1:12–14)

Discuss:

What inspiring examples have you seen of men and women working together using their God-given gifts?

Threats

But we don't always work together to fulfill God's purposes. Sometimes, we see our allies as threats. Ironically, the story of Adam and Eve has been used to undermine the alliance between men and women. Often Eve is described as easily deceived, manipulative, and representative of all women. This interpretation teaches that Adam's sin was not only in wanting to be like God, but in listening to a woman and following her lead.[5]

First Timothy 2, which references Adam and Eve, has often been interpreted as a prohibition on women teaching men. It's true that if the Ephesian women who Paul mentions were teachers, they would have threatened the church's doctrine! But does that mean women should never teach? If we take a closer look, we find Paul telling us how Eve's story ends—and what that means for our churches today.

We will base our exegesis on the method we outlined in our first session. First, let's set some **literary context** for 1 Timothy:

Read: 1 Timothy 1:1–7, 18–20, 3:15

What genre is this writing?

Who is writing to whom?

Why? (Host, check out my findings at the bottom of the next page.)

 Read: 1 Timothy 2:1–15

 Explore:

Underline every word that is repeated in this passage (you can group concepts together too, like "come to knowledge," "learn" and "teacher").

Then, break the passage into sections. What is the emphasis of each section?

Using the repeated words as clues, how do the sections relate to each other? How do they relate to Paul's theme of false teachers?

What seems to be Paul's overall concern? (I've included what I found at the bottom of the next page—you can read that instead if you don't have time).

Who were the false teachers?[6]
The biggest threat to the Ephesian church had to do with false teaching and women.[7] He warns Timothy against "godless myths and old wives' tales" (1 Tim. 4:7). It seems that false teachers such as Hymenaeus and Alexander (1:19-20) were deceiving women in the Ephesian church. Young widows were going from house to house, talking nonsense and saying things they ought not to say (5:13). Some had turned away to follow Satan (5:15).

The false teachers wanted to teach their own doctrine but were unwilling to learn from the appointed church leaders. Paul "handed [the two men] over to Satan to be taught not to blaspheme" (1:19).

However, the women who had been influenced by the teachers could still be part of the Christian community. The deceived women should not try to assume the authority of teachers in the church (2:12), but should, like good students of their day, submit to recognized teachers.[8] Their legitimate need for knowledge should be addressed. Paul instructs Timothy that they should learn proper church doctrine (2:11). In fact, "should learn" is the only command verb (imperative) in the passage.[9]

The Woman and Jesus[10]

The situation reminded Paul of how Eve was deceived by the first false teacher—the snake—who misled her about the knowledge of good and evil and persuaded her to grasp for unauthorized authority (2:13-14).[11] As a result of Eve's sin, God said, "with painful labor you will give birth to children" (Gen. 3:16).

However, God promised that the negative consequences would be reversed. A child born by a woman would crush the head of the snake (Gen. 3:15). Women would be saved by the birth of the child—Jesus (1 Tim. 2:15).[12]

Answers: Read: 1 Timothy 1:1–7, 18–20, 3:15
Paul is writing a personal letter to his spiritual "son" Timothy, whom he left in charge of the church in Ephesus (1 Tim. 1:1–2). Paul writes to instruct Timothy on how to refute false teaching in the growing Ephesian church (1:3) and teach him "how people ought to conduct themselves in God's household" (3:15).

Answers: Explore
First instruction: "I urge. . . that. . . prayers be made for all people," especially authority (vv. 1–2). Reasoning: "we may live peaceful and quiet lives in all godliness and holiness" (v. 2), God "wants all people to be saved and come to a knowledge of truth" (vv. 1–4), God is one (vv. 5–6).

Defense: Paul is telling the truth. . . a true (not false) teacher with authority to give instructions (v. 7).

Second instruction: If you worship God, act like it (v.10). Men should "pray, lifting up holy hands without anger or disputing" (v. 8). Women should not show off their wealth (gold, pearls, expensive clothes), but their good deeds (vv. 9–10).

Third instruction: A woman should "learn in quietness" not "teach or assume authority. . . she must be quiet" (vv. 11–12). Reasoning: Adam and Eve (vv. 13–14), "women will be saved. . . if they continue in. . . holiness with propriety" (v. 15). Paul is concerned for the holiness and salvation of all people, which were under threat from false teaching in Ephesus. The crucial relationships between God, men, and women were crumbling. Men were angry and arguing and women were showing off their wealth (gold, pearls, and expensive clothes) rather than their good deeds. They were not talking to God enough in prayer or listening to each other.

The Savior was brought into the world by a unique trio: God's spirit inside a woman (Mary), with the support of a man (Joseph - see Luke

Curious about this explanation? **Dig deeper** by checking out the endnotes in this session.

1:26–38, Matt. 1:18–25). Through his life, death and resurrection, Jesus restored people's relationship with God and each other. Despite Adam and Eve's rebellion, Jesus overcame sin and its consequences. Though the snake deceived, accused, and brought death, Jesus crushed the serpent's head. He is the truth and the life (John 14:6). He mediates our forgiveness (Rom. 8:33–34) and gives us new life (1 Cor. 15:55–56). He says, "I have come so that they may have life and have it in abundance" (John 10:10 HCSB).

Paul reminds these women that even though they were deceived, if they demonstrated their faith in Jesus through lives of holiness and love, they too would be saved.

In summary: To counter the threat in the Ephesian church, Paul reminded Timothy of the alliance that had been broken by deception. He urged Timothy to stay away from false teaching (1 Tim. 4:7, 6:20) and teach truth (4:13), even to women. Equipping men and women in the church with sound doctrine would strengthen the alliance, furthering God's goal of all people being saved and knowing the truth.[13]

Paul and his women allies

However, not all women in the church in Paul's day lacked training in the truth. In fact, Paul recognized several women as teachers and commended these ministry allies.[14] Paul wrote to his spiritual son Timothy that he valued Lois and Eunice as partners in nurturing Timothy's faith:

> I am reminded of your sincere faith, which first lived in your grandmother Lois and in your mother Eunice and, I am persuaded, now lives in you also. For this reason I remind you to fan into flames the gift that is in you through the laying on of my hands. (2 Timothy 1:5)

 Read: Acts 18:1–4, 18–19, 24–28

Paul called Priscilla a co-worker in Christ Jesus, and often Priscilla's name is often mentioned before her husband's, suggesting her prominence (Rom. 16:3–4, 2 Tim. 4:19). After being taught by Paul, she instructed Apollos, whose teaching greatly influenced the Corinthian church, among others (1 Cor. 3:4–9).

 Read: Romans 16:1–16

Paul commends several women in the Roman church, including Phoebe, "a deacon of the Church in Cenchreae;" Priscilla and her husband; and Junia, who was "outstanding among the apostles" along with her husband.[15]

Paul also would have known about Mary's influence on the early church.

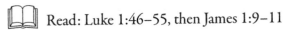 Read: Luke 1:46–55, then James 1:9–11

Mary, the mother of Jesus and James (who wrote the book of James), had a strong influence on her sons' upbringing, and that would have included teaching them. The themes of her song shape James' introduction to his book. Luke 1-2 contains information such as the angel Gabriel's words to Mary, which only Mary would have known. This means that at some point, she told the nativity story to Luke or someone he interviewed.

 Discuss:

How have people of the opposite gender (of any age) blessed your life?

What tasks have you been given as God's ally? Which other people are you an ally for?

Love God, Love Neighbor
Throughout the Old and New Testaments, women were used by God as allies in with men to teach God's people, advocate for the disadvantaged, and sustain life.

Today, Jesus works amid the community of Christians—the church—to continue his mission of bringing salvation, reconciliation and truth to the world. Together, men and women in the church community reveal to the world what God is like; we humans are God's image on earth.

In order to accomplish the missions that God has given us, we must keep our alliance intact. In fact, acting out of love for God and others is one way that we reflect the truth that we are made in God's image:

> This is how we know that we live in [God] and he in us: He has given us of his Spirit. And we have seen and testify that the Father has sent his Son to be the Savior of the world... We love because he first loved us... Anyone who loves God must also love their brother and sister. (1 John 4:13–14, 19, 21)

 Watch:

"Love God, Love Neighbor" by FTE
(cbe.today/goodnews)

God still asks us image-bearers to show our love for God by caring for creation and each other (John 15:10-12). Jesus has reversed the deadly effects of sin in our world, saving people physically and spiritually. Now we're invited to be part of God's saving power in people's lives – it's a big job! But the Holy Spirit is a powerful ally. God has also equipped us with love and the gift of each other in our church community. Our alliance can accomplish more than we imagine possible. Together, may we join in God's mission of bringing life in abundance.

 Pray:

Father, Son and Holy Spirit, together you created all life and beauty. We're made in your image—what an honor! Yet sometimes we still doubt your goodness. We try to be like gods and turn against our allies. Thank you for forgiving and rescuing us. Empower us to love you and love each other.

 Sing:

"Build your Kingdom Here"
by Rend Collective Experiment, 2012
(cbe.today/goodnews)

Come set your rule and reign
in our hearts again

Increase in us we pray
Unveil why we're made
Come set our hearts ablaze with hope
like wildfire in our very souls
Holy Spirit, come invade us now
We are your church
We need your power in us

We seek your kingdom first
We hunger and we thirst
Refuse to waste our lives
for you're our joy and prize
To see the captive hearts released
The hurt, the sick, the poor at peace
We lay down our lives for heaven's cause

Pre-chorus:
We are your church
We pray revive this earth

Chorus:
Build your kingdom here
Let the darkness fear
Show your mighty hand
Heal our streets and land
Set your church on fire
Win this nation back
Change the atmosphere
Build your kingdom here
We pray

Unleash your kingdom's power
reaching the near and far.
No force of hell can stop
your beauty changing hearts.
You made us for much more than this!
Awake the kingdom seed in us!

Fill us with the strength and love of Christ.
Pre-chorus
Chorus x2

 Challenge: Pray the prayer of *examen*

The prayer of *examen* is a spiritual discipline where you reflect on the positive and negative parts of the day and look for God's presence. Before the next session, examine your relationships with the opposite gender and with God. Create a quiet atmosphere, perhaps in nature or with a candle. You may want to close your eyes. Ask yourself what you are most and least grateful for in these relationships. When have you been most or least able to give and receive love? Say thank you for the relationships God has given you as gifts. Confess broken areas of criticism, fear, or shame. Breathe deeply. Reflect on how God loves you and others, even when we don't love each other.

For further reflection, you can write a letter of thanks or confession. Address it to God, yourself or someone else. If it's appropriate, send the letter.

Come back to the group ready to share what you learned about how our relationships with God and people are intertwined.

 Go:

Until we meet again, let us give thanks for God and each other, our allies in renewing creation.

 Learn more:

Half the Sky by Nicholas Kristof and Sheryl WuDunn
Mao Zedong said, "women hold up half the sky," a concept that connects closely to the idea of a trio between men, women and God. This book, coauthored by a man and a woman, began a movement that empowers women, especially rural women without access to basic literacy and healthcare, to be part of changing the world's problems. Learn more about the movement: (cbe.today/goodnews).

Half the Church by Carolyn Custis James

Carolyn Custis James responds to "Half the Sky." Since the church is the agent of healing to the world, she urges the church to use the gifts of all their members - including the female half. She describes how men and women work together build God's kingdom. If you're curious, check out the trailer for her book: (cbe.today/goodnews).

Powerful Love in the Body

❝ Submit to one another out of reverence for Christ.**❞**
Ephesians 5:21

 Challenge Check-in:

Can you say last session's theme verse?

What was the prayer of examen like for you?

 Explore:

What is your favorite parody, takeoff, or satire?

What makes something a good spoof?

 Watch:

Ask if one or two group members have an example of a parody or spoof that they can easily show the group (a song, music video, fake news article, image etc.) We'll come back to the idea of parody later in the session.

The Marriage Alliance

We talked last time about how God uses men and women working together in a variety of relationships to accomplish God's purposes. For this session, we'll focus on the marriage alliance. One of the most famous Bible passages about marriage is in Paul's letter to the Ephesians. Let's use some of our exegesis skills to uncover Paul's cleverly communicated message:

📖 Read: Ephesians 5:21–6:9

You may be thinking, "This passage seems straightforward. We have parents, children, husbands, and wives today. Can't we skip looking at the context?" But Paul implies that families in the Ephesian church also had slaves. We can't assume that the part about slaves doesn't apply to us, but the expectations for husband-wife and parent-child relationships that Paul's talking about match our cultures today.[1] We should be cautious of interpretations that apply one verse of the Bible word-for-word and then dismiss the relevance of the next verse.

Let's examine the **cultural context** of the Roman Empire, specifically for marriage relationships.[2] A man often married a woman 12–15 years younger than himself. Parents often arranged their children's marriages.[3] How does this compare to your culture? Paul was writing to a church where a typical wealthy man had a wife, had many children, and often slaves. This kind of man had uncontested power over his subordinates. The man's power was supported by the laws of the state, and, according to their philosophers, the laws of nature too.

Let's return to our exegesis questions, this time focusing on the **literary context** of the passage:

What is the structure of the passage? Paul gives general instruction (v. 21) and then applies it to three specific relationships. Paul addresses the societally subordinate member of each pair first.[4]

What is the genre of the passage? Paul is writing a letter to the Ephesians, but in 5:21–6:9, he evokes another well-known genre of the time, the Greco-Roman household code.[5]

From Aristotle onward, Greco-Roman culture followed household codes, or advice books that instructed heads-of-households on how to manage

Curious about Aristotle's advice? **Dig deeper** at the back of the book.

their property, slaves, children, and wives.[6] Men were expected to instruct their subordinates. But these advice books never told men how to behave. Men were supposed to preside over the household rather than being considered part of it. Paul imitates Aristotle's household code by discussing wives, children, and slaves. But Paul treats these subordinates very differently than Aristotle. Ephesians 5 is a parody. By using the same literary structure, Paul acknowledges existing structures of power so he can directly comment on how Christian households are radically different.

Paul still asks wives, children, and slaves to respect the head-of-household's authority. What's surprising is that Paul talks directly to the subservient member of each pair, treating them as a person who is responsible for their own choices, rather than simply under the rule of a male head-of-household.[7] Paul also changes their motivation. They are not required to submit or obey because nature made them inferior to those with power. Their submission is actually to God alone, who created all people to reflect the image of deity. Not only that, God gives obedient children long life (Eph. 6:2–3) and diligent slaves a heavenly reward (Eph. 6:8). Paul encourages these people to continue honoring their husbands/fathers/masters—but now from a Christian motivation of obeying God and serving others.

Next, Paul gives advice to the men themselves—three times. He explains that part of managing their affairs has to do with managing their own conduct. Maybe the men of Ephesus thought that when Paul said, "Submit to one another out of reverence for Christ," he meant they only had to submit to other men of similar status. So Paul makes himself clear. Submitting and love are not only for people of equal status.[8] All Christians, men included, must submit to one another. Elsewhere he says Christians are to be "enslaved" to one another.[9] Here he says that Christian men submit in love even to their slaves.

Body Partners
After addressing slaves, Paul turns to their masters, saying, "in the same way" (Eph. 5:9). This signals that his instruction to slaves and masters and husbands and wives are different ways of expressing the same idea. So, how different are the commands to husbands and wives?

Husbands are told to love their wives as their own body (Eph. 5:28–30). He tells wives that they should submit because the husband is the head of the wife (Eph. 5:23–24). The creation story tells us that wives and husbands are part of one body. Eve was taken out of Adam's side. Now when a man and woman marry, they become "one flesh" again (Gen. 2:21–24). (We'll talk more about how exactly man is the head of woman next session.)

Paul also uses the image of Christ and the church joined together as one body to emphasize that in Christian marriage, wives and husbands are united in the body of Christ as well. This is why Christians should treat their spouses with the same care that they treat their own body.

🎵 Sing:

"The Servant Song"
by Richard Gillard, 1977
(Final verse by Steven and Janice Rasmussen for their wedding)
(cbe.today/goodnews)

Brother, let me be your servant
Let me be as Christ to you
Pray that I might have the grace to
Let you be my servant too.

Sister, let me be your servant
Let me be as Christ to you
Pray that I might have the grace to
Let you be my servant too.

We are pilgrims on a journey
We are partners on the road
We are here to help each other
Walk the mile and bear the load.

I will hold the Christ-light for you
In the night time of your fear.

I will hold my hand out to you;
Speak the peace you long to hear.

I will weep when you are weeping
When you laugh I'll laugh with you
I will share your joys and sorrows
'Til we've seen this journey though.

When we sing to God in heaven
We shall find such harmony
Born of all we've known together
Of Christ's love and agony.

Jesus, let us be your servants
Let us serve your world for you
May they know that you have loved us
And you want to love them too.

One Body

Paul builds his code of conduct for Christian households from the foundational truths he laid out in the previous chapter, such as the truth that Christians are one body united to one Master (Lord):

> Make every effort to keep the bond of unity of the Spirit through the bond of peace. There is one body and one Spirit, just as you were called to one hope when you were called; one Lord, one faith, one baptism; one God who is over all and through all and in all. (Ephesians 4:3–6)

Everything changes when we are members of one body—either as wives and husbands or as members of a church body. If your stomach is hungry and tells you to feed it, you obey. If your legs are tired, the rest of the body cares for them by sitting down. You listen to your body's needs and address them out of love—because the good of all your body parts is affected by the wellbeing of one part. In our physical bodies, this kind of submission of one part to another makes sense, because the whole body is more important than its parts. The same is true in the body of Christ, the church.

Love and Obey

In the New Testament as a whole, loving and submitting to each other are not commands for husbands or wives alone. They are the same as instructions given to men and women as church members. For example, earlier in Ephesians, Paul talks about how Christ is the head of the church—all Christians (Eph. 1:22–23)—and how all Christians are called to love as Christ loved us (Eph. 4:32–5:2). Paul calls Christians to submit to one another at the beginning of this passage (Eph. 5:21) and in another letter (Phil. 2:1–11). Jesus asks everyone to love others as themselves (Matt. 22:39).

Jesus also says that loving him is the same as obeying him (John 14:15, 21, 23). The greatest love of all is to lay down one's life for a friend (John 15:10–13). Jesus laid down his life for us in submission to the Father. We can show our love for Jesus by submitting our lives to him. Freely doing the will of someone else shows that we know and care about what they desire.

Wives are not the only people called to submit or obey. Husbands are not the only people called to love and lay down their lives. All church members are called to submit to one another, to love each other, to obey Christ, and to lay down their lives for him! Paul emphasizes that Christian spouses should especially apply these attitudes to their marriages because Christian spouses are part of one body both through the church and through marriage.

 Discuss:

How did you feel about Ephesians 5 before this study? How might you see things differently now?

From your observation or experience, what might respectful and loving submission look like in marriage?

Submitting to Authority

We worship Christ by sacrificing our bodies to do God's will (Rom. 12:1–2) and by submitting to each other. First, we are to submit to institutions God has put in place over us and willingly serve them:

Read: 1 Peter 2:11–17

Christianity becomes attractive to non-believers when Christians have a reputation for loving each other and respecting civic authority (unless the authorities ask us to disobey God). In our lives today, we too must strive to "show proper respect to everyone [and] love the family of believers," knowing that it is God's orders we choose to obey.[10]

 Discuss:

What prevents you from doing the will of authorities, of those you love, or of God?

The Power of a Servant

Next, Paul challenges those in positions of power and privilege to realize that in the kingdom of God, they must be the first to serve others.

Often the person who loves the least in a relationship has the most power to selfishly control the actions of the other person.[11] In contrast, God's power is always expressed through love. Because the members of the Trinity love each other, they serve each other. Because God loved humanity more than his own power (John 3:16), Jesus became a servant and dwelled as a human (Phil. 2:7). Rather than accusing others, Jesus accepted blame for the sins of others, conquering sin.

Let's read Jesus' first public statement about his mission.

 Read: Luke 4:18–19

God is far more powerful than any wealthy Ephesian man. But Jesus became human like us. He spent time with lepers, prostitutes, tax collectors, women, foreigners and the poor. He said, "It is not the healthy who need a doctor, but the sick" (Mark 2:17). The poor, he said, will inherit the kingdom of heaven (Matt. 5:3). He used his miraculous power to help the powerless.

True Religion

As Jesus' followers, we are invited to follow his example. Most of us have some kind of power. Rather than lording our privilege over others, we can advocate for those with less power, empathize with their lives and serve them. We should be suspicious of any teaching or practice that favors the powerful or associates Christianity with status. To measure our own love, we should examine how we treat the poor and vulnerable, because we have no earthly incentive to treat them well. James explains:

> Religion that God our Father accepts as pure and faultless is this: to look after orphans and widows in their distress and to keep oneself from being polluted by the world... Has not God chosen those who are poor in the eyes of the world to be rich in faith and to inherit the kingdom he promised those who love him? (James 1:27, 2:5)

It's tempting to grasp for power and only value people in positions of influence. But the Bible flips our perspective upside-down. "Moving up" in God's kingdom means bending down: in worship of God, in submission to legitimate authorities, and in service to the less powerful. This upside-down orientation makes sense when we realize we are part of one body through marriage or through the church. Selfishness gives way to service as the whole body experiences the pain, delight, and needs of each part.

 Discuss:

> What would it look like if our community actually cared about other people as much as our own bodies—their suffering, imprisonment (Heb. 13:3), nakedness, hunger, or sickness?

What prevents you from advocating for the powerless?

 Pray:

Lord Jesus, enable us to love you by obeying you. Teach us your selfless love. In marriage and the church, may we put the rest of the body before ourselves. It's hard for us to love the poor without disdaining the authorities, or vice versa. We need your help to live in your upside-down kingdom.

 Challenge: Use your power to serve

As a group, ask God to open your eyes and heart to those who have less power in your community. Spend several minutes listening in silence. Then, before the next session, ask people in your community if there are organizations or people serving the community who you or your friends could join. Or, ask whether your group could help with umet needs in your community. Come back to the group ready to plan how you will serve together as the body.

 Go:

Until we meet again, let us humbly love and serve other parts of the body.

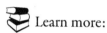 Learn more:

Red Letter Revolution: What if Jesus Really Meant What He Said? by Shane Claiborne and Tony Campolo
Claiborne and Campolo challenge Christians to embody Jesus' words—in economics, politics, and social issues—and see what God does. They share a concern for Christians giving up power to live among and serve the poor, but have lived out their commitments differently as members of different generations. In addition to the book they wrote together, their website hosts videos and blog posts for ongoing conversation about how we can follow Jesus: (cbe.today/goodnews).

UNIT 3
Our Calling

We are all members of Christ's body and followers of Jesus. We need each other to inspire and equip other people to follow Jesus.

To discover this, we look at the historical and cultural context of Scripture and apply it to our lives. We also dig into profiles of Bible characters and ask how our stories connect with theirs.

Build the Body

" Instead, speaking the truth in love, we will grow to become in every respect the mature body of him who is the head, that is, Christ. From him the whole body, joined and held together by every supporting ligament, grows and builds itself up in love, as each part does its work. "
Ephesians 4:15–16

 Challenge Check-in:

Can you say last session's theme verse?

What ideas do you have for how the group can serve the less powerful?

Choose someone to finalize plans for your group to serve the community.

Covering the Head
Throughout these sessions, Paul has been one of our main informants about God. We've discovered that God includes Gentiles, turns power structures upside-down and lives within and among people.

So when Paul says, "The head of every man is Christ, and the head of the woman is man, and the head of Christ is God," it poses a problem (1 Cor. 11:3). This seems to introduce hierarchy into the Trinity and into the alliance between men and women. It seems to create three heads and therefore three bodies rather than one. What is going on here? Do some members of Christ's body have special authority over others?

What could this passage have to teach us about building up the body?

📖 Read: 1 Corinthians 11:2–16

To try to understand what Paul is saying, let's ask our exegesis questions about the **literary context**:

What genre is this writing?

Who is writing to whom?

Why? (See my answers at the bottom of the page.)

Next, let's look at the **cultural context**:

For now, let's just cover the cultural context of the word head. In our first session, we gave an example of how "LOL" might mean "lots of love" or "laugh out loud" depending on your generation. In this passage, the way we understand the word "head" is different from how Jewish and Greek authors used it. English speakers talk about the head of an organization or a household as the authority figure. Because of our modern scientific understanding of the brain, we think of the head of the body as the rational command center of the body.[1] But in New Testament times, the heart was seen as the rational center of the body, while the kidneys were seen as the seat of the emotions.[2]

So what did head mean?[3]

Greek literature usually used the word "head" to describe the source of something, similar to how in English we would describe the "headwaters" of a river.[4] For Jews, the "head of the year" is Rosh Hashanah, the Jewish New Year." The rest of the year flows from its head, just as wisdom comes from fearing the Lord. In Genesis 1:1, "In the beginning" uses the same root as the Hebrew word for head.[5]

Paul is writing a letter of instruction to the church in the city of Corinth. He was responding to an earlier letter sent by the Corinthian church, as well as reports of divisions and immorality (especially sexual immorality) among them. For more, see "Introduction: 1 Corinthians" in W. Harold Mare, "1 Corinthians" in *The NIV Study Bible, 2011*, ed. Kenneth L. Barker (Grand Rapids: Zondervan, 2011), 1919–1923."

Where do you come from?

With this understanding, we realize that Paul is telling the story of creation and the incarnation.

 Read:

Paul references other parts of the Bible. Let's weave these threads together. Ask four people designated "A," "B", "C" and "D" to read these verses. Listen to how each story picks up on themes in the other passages. If you have five people, you can split the B part into B1 and B2.

> A: In the beginning was the Word, and the Word was with God, and the Word was God. He was with God in the beginning. Through him all things were made; without him nothing was made that has been made. (John 1:1–3)

> B: The head [source] of every man is Christ. (1 Cor. 11:3)

> C: The LORD God formed a man [*adam* in Hebrew] from the dust of the ground [*adamah* in Hebrew] and breathed into his nostrils the breath of life, and the man became a living being. (Gen. 2:7)⁶

> C: This is the written account of Adam's family line. When God created mankind [adam], he made them in the likeness of God. He created them male and female and blessed them. And he named them "Mankind" [*adam*] when they were created. (Gen. 5:1–2)⁷

> B2: Man is the image and glory of God. (1 Cor. 11:7)

> B: The head [source] of every woman is the man. (1 Cor. 11:3)

> B2: Woman is the glory [but not the image]⁸ of man. For man did not come from woman, but woman from man, neither was man created for woman, but woman for man... (1 Cor. 11:7)

> C: The LORD God said, "It is not good for the man to be alone. I will make a helper suitable for him." . . . So the man gave names to all the livestock, the birds in the sky and all the wild animals. But for Adam [the man] no suitable helper was found. So the LORD God caused the man to fall into a deep sleep; and while he was sleeping, he took one of the man's ribs [or part of the man's side] and then closed

up the place with flesh. Then the LORD God made a woman from the rib [or part] he had taken out of the man, and he brought her to the man. The man said, "This is now bone of my bones and flesh of my flesh; she shall be called 'woman' for she was taken out of man." (Gen. 2:18, 20–23)

B2: Nevertheless, in the Lord woman is not independent of man, nor is man independent of woman. For as woman came from man, so also man is born of woman. (1 Cor. 11:11–12)

C: Adam named his wife Eve, because she would become the mother of all the living... Adam made love to his wife Eve, and she became pregnant and gave birth to Cain. She said, "With the help of the LORD I have brought forth a man." When Adam had lived 130 years, he had a son in his own likeness, in his own image; and he named him Seth. (Gen. 3:20, 4:1, 5:3)

B2: But everything [man and woman] comes from God. (1 Cor. 11:12b)

B: And the head [source] of Christ is the Godhead. (1 Cor. 11:3)

D: The Holy Spirit descended on [Jesus] like a dove. And a voice came from heaven: "You are my Son, whom I love; with you I am well pleased." ...[Jesus] was the son, so it was thought of Joseph [tracing Joseph's genealogy back through Joseph, Jesus is still] the son of God." (Luke 3:22–23, 38)

A: "The Word became flesh and made his dwelling among us. We have seen his glory, the glory of the one and only Son, who came from the Father, full of grace and truth." (John 1:14)

In summary: Since Paul is talking about covering the head, he uses the metaphor of a head in the sense of source to describe the relationships between God, Christ, men and women.[9] In creation, man came from Christ and woman came from man (Eve from Adam). But now, men come from women (their mothers). In the incarnation, Christ came from God.[10]

 For a diagram of Paul's symmetry, **dig deeper** at the back of the book.

Paul is saying that the Trinity is interdependent, and men and women also depend on each other for life. In fact, Paul uses a symmetrical structure to balance each statement about men with a statement about women.[11] He emphasizes that man and woman are each other's counterpart and they need each other to be fruitful. No part of Christ's body can make it alone. Both genders need each other to respectfully build up the church through prayer and prophecy. We need to honor each other and the Godhead through our worship.

Jesus' Body

In the next chapter, Paul moves from discussing "head" to explore how all people are united to one another because they are joined to Christ—the head of the church.

 Read: 1 Corinthians 12:4–31

In summary: Paul emphasizes that spiritual gifts all come from the same God and have the same purpose of building up the church body (vv. 4–6). Therefore, each person is an important body part with a purpose (v. 27). Our goal is not competition or comparison. Paul doesn't specify which people correspond to different body parts, but he does say that even the head needs the rest of the body (v. 21). In fact, "those parts of the body that seem to be weaker are indispensable, and the parts of the body that we think are less honorable we treat with special honor" (vv. 22–23).

Watch:

Juanita Bynum sings "I Need You to Survive" with a gospel choir and orchestra (cbe.today/goodnews).

The lyrics of this song express the interdependence of men and women (1 Cor. 11:11) and of all members of the body (1 Cor. 12:21, 26). To create this kind of performance, people of different races and genders needed each other. Each voice is needed in the gospel choir, each instrument in the orchestra.

Your Part

Discovering your spiritual gifts requires more than a personality test. You develop gifts as you obey the Spirit in a variety of circumstances, learning from others in your community. God gives each of us spiritual gifts not only to know more about ourselves but in order to help others know God (v. 13). God can also give multiple gifts to someone or can give different gifts at different times in life, according to what the church body needs. We build Christ's body as we devote our bodies to living sacrificially for God:

 Read: Romans 12:1–8

 Explore:

Let's look at the seven spiritual gifts listed in Romans 12. Each person can learn about a gift (or gifts) by reading the following descriptions and looking up the Bible stories where women and men exemplify these gifts. Then present what you learn about each gift to each other. Just for fun, these gifts have each been matched up with a body part (based on today's understanding of the body!). For an extra challenge, try to emphasize the related body part in creative ways throughout the presentation.[12]

Men and women of many backgrounds and gifts have contributed to God's mission throughout history.

Prophets can deliver any message God wants to give people, not just predictions of future events. God can ask prophets to live in radical ways to make a statement about how society needs to change.

Servants see needs and enjoy filling them. They may run errands, build, clean, garden, create hand-made items, repair electronics, cook, or offer rides. Their behind-the-scenes work is often underappreciated.

Teachers enjoy asking questions and thinking critically. They love bringing others along in a journey of understanding. While this may include Bible study, they can teach in many areas of life.

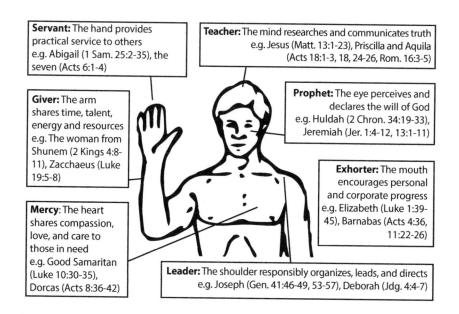

Servant: The hand provides practical service to others e.g. Abigail (1 Sam. 25:2-35), the seven (Acts 6:1-4)

Teacher: The mind researches and communicates truth e.g. Jesus (Matt. 13:1-23), Priscilla and Aquila (Acts 18:1-3, 18, 24-26, Rom. 16:3-5)

Giver: The arm shares time, talent, energy and resources e.g. The woman from Shunem (2 Kings 4:8-11), Zacchaeus (Luke 19:5-8)

Prophet: The eye perceives and declares the will of God e.g. Huldah (2 Chron. 34:19-33), Jeremiah (Jer. 1:4-12, 13:1-11)

Exhorter: The mouth encourages personal and corporate progress e.g. Elizabeth (Luke 1:39-45), Barnabas (Acts 4:36, 11:22-26)

Mercy: The heart shares compassion, love, and care to those in need e.g. Good Samaritan (Luke 10:30-35), Dorcas (Acts 8:36-42)

Leader: The shoulder responsibly organizes, leads, and directs e.g. Joseph (Gen. 41:46-49, 53-57), Deborah (Jdg. 4:4-7)

Exhorters envision possibilities and work to make them reality. They are dedicated to their own improvement. They mentor, challenge, and encourage other people to achieve their potential.

Givers find joy in generosity. They may enjoy giving hugs, hosting groups at their homes, donating to charity, volunteering their professional skills, or buying presents for friends.

Leaders carry the weight of tasks on their shoulders. They see the big picture and feel responsible to accomplish goals. They delegate tasks and administrate logistics.

People with the **mercy** gift empathize easily. They are good listeners and withhold judgment of the needy. Others may seek them out when struggling with addiction, financial stress, or pain.

The gifts are people

 Read: Ephesians 4:1–16

In summary: Believers are united (vv. 1–6) but we all live out our calling according to the grace God gives each of us (v. 7). Notice that in this passage, Paul doesn't talk about the gift of prophecy or teaching—he says the people themselves are gifts from Christ to equip God's people (v. 12). Just as you need others, others need you for the body to reach maturity (v. 15). No part of the body can take pride in being more important than the rest.

God is three-in-one—a united God expressed in a diversity of ways. Creation reveals that its Maker delights in diversity. In the same way, the body of Christ has many different parts. When we work together, our multifaceted community reflects the Creator's beauty. We cannot reflect God's design alone. We cannot accomplish God's mission for the church alone. We all need each other in the body.

 Discuss:

What gifts do you see in other members of this group? Affirm each other for how you each build up the body, using specific examples if possible.

Allow each person to respond. Do you see these (or other) gifts in yourself?

How have you been using your gift(s) or how would you like to do so? What challenges are involved?

What needs and opportunities do you notice in the body? Could you or someone else in the group fill this?

 Sing:

"I Need You to Survive"
by Hezekiah Walker, 2004
(cbe.today/goodnews)

I need you, you need me.
We're all a part of God's body.
Stand with me, agree with me.
We're all a part of God's body.

It is his will that every need be supplied
You are important to me, I need you to survive
(Repeat 3x)

I pray for you, you pray for me
I love you, I need you to survive
I won't harm you with words from my mouth
I love you, I need you to survive
(Repeat 8x)

It is his will that every need be supplied
You are important to me, I need you to survive

 Pray:

God, you are the source of all good things. Thank you for giving us your Spirit, expressed differently through each of us. Protect us against pride and insecurity, which tell us some people are more important than others. Christ, as members of your body, we all need each other. Help us to build each other up.

 Challenge: Find a Mentor

Before the next session, seek out a spiritual mentor—someone you connect with or who has a gift you'd like to grown in. Ask if this person would be willing to meet regularly to discuss your spiritual growth. As a conversation starter, you may wish to read the whole of Romans 12 together and discuss ways to build the body of the church. Come back to the group ready to share your first steps in building the body.

 Go:

Until we meet again, let us build each other up in the church.

 Learn more:

Creating a Missional Culture by J. R. Woodward
J. R. Woodward equips Christian leaders of all ages to discover and use the gifts God has given them to serve the rest of the body. Our call is to

mission—outward engagement with the culture. Woodward instructs leaders on how to inspire and mentor others toward becoming focused on God's mission as a community.

Equipped for Every Good Work: Building a Gifts-Based Church by Dan R. Dick and Barbara A. Dick
This practical book leads a congregation through a process of discovering each member's spiritual gift, how they lead and interact with others, how they experience God, and what kind of tasks they enjoy doing. The authors' goal is to empower churches to engage their members in the service God has already equipped them for.

Follow and Make Followers

> **"** Whoever wants to be my disciple must deny themselves
> and take up their cross daily and follow me. **"**
> Luke 9:23

 Challenge Check-in:

Can you say last session's theme verse?

Who have you found as a potential mentor? What challenges are you facing?

If you've already had a chance to serve your community, what was it like? If not, what are your final plans?

Explore:

Ask each person to think of a famous person whose mannerisms they can imitate. Then, take turns acting like your character while the group guesses who you are. Instead of talking about your character ("I'm a pop singer"), adopt that person's voice, body language, and topics of speech. Vote for most accurate and most hilarious!

Who leads, who follows?

 Discuss:

When you think of leading, what do you think of? What about following?

Does being a man or woman affect whether people expect someone to lead or follow? In which situations?

As we've discussed what the Bible teaches us about gender, we've talked about the many ways that God values and uses men and women of any background equally. We've seen that the alliance between men and women is important, and that the body of Christ needs every part's contribution—even if your gift is leadership and you're a woman.

But regardless of whether God calls you to lead, the Bible has another, more exciting call for women and men: "Follow me."

You may be thinking, "Following is boring. Have you ever heard of conferences or manuals about followership?" It's true that the world prizes leadership. But in the upside-down kingdom, following is the secret to adventure.

In the first five books of the Bible, God gives Israel comprehensive instructions. God talks about what or who the Israelites should follow thirteen times more frequently than he commands them to lead![1]

 Read: Deuteronomy 4:10–14

God called all Israelites to follow him through the wilderness, leading them with a pillar of cloud or of fire (Ex. 13:21). God called all Israelites to follow the Law he gave them. If they obeyed, God would bless them richly. If they followed other gods, God would punish them (Deut. 28). Some Israelites, like Moses, were also called to lead others. But they were to lead others in following God, not themselves.

Follow Me
But Israel could not follow God's laws fully. So God decided to let them follow a person—Jesus, the fulfillment and embodiment of the law.

Jesus began his ministry by becoming a follower, or a disciple, of his cousin, John the Baptist:

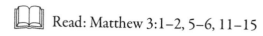 Read: Matthew 3:1–2, 5–6, 11–15

The next day, one of John's disciples, Andrew, told his brother Simon Peter: "We have found the Messiah!" (John 1:35–42).

When Simon Peter and his fishermen companions followed Jesus' unconventional fishing instructions, they caught so many fish their nets began to break (Luke 5:1–10). "Come, follow me," Jesus said to Simon Peter, "and I will send you out to fish for people" (Matt. 4:19). Religious teachers never invited uneducated people like fishermen to be disciples. These fishermen knew this was the offer of a lifetime. "So they pulled their boats up on shore, left everything and followed him" (Luke 5:11).

Some **cultural context** is helpful here. Many Jewish teachers in Jesus' day had their own disciples. The goal of a disciple was to become exactly like his teacher. First, the teacher baptized a disciple as a symbol of the disciple's allegiance. As the teacher went from town to town teaching, the disciple studied his teacher. He copied the teacher's mannerisms and actions. He internalized the teacher's interpretations. A disciple was not allowed to write down their teacher's words, because he was expected to memorized them—showing the teacher's words had entered the student's heart and affected his life. Finally, he transmitted his master's teachings to a new generation of disciples.[2]

You couldn't just become a disciple. A teacher had to choose you. The words "Follow me" were a recognized formal invitation to a new relationship, like the words "Will you marry me?"[3] Accepting the offer was a major commitment—and a huge privilege.

 Discuss:

How does the description of discipleship in Jesus' day challenge you?

Simon Peter: Is This the Way?
Simon Peter discovered that Jesus was unlike any other teacher.

Jesus washed his disciples' feet. Peter initially would not allow Jesus to wash his feet, just like the John the Baptist initially refused to baptize Jesus. How shameful for a leader to act like a servant! But afterwards Jesus explained, "You call me 'Teacher' and 'Lord,' and rightly so, for that is what I am. Now that I, your Lord and Teacher, have washed your feet, you also should wash one another's feet" (John 13:13–14). Yes, washing feet was beneath a Rabbi's job description, but humble service fit perfectly with the character of God incarnate. And if the master serves people, how much more should his servants!

Leadership according to Jesus meant suffering and service:

> Jesus called [the disciples] together and said, "You know that the rulers of the Gentiles lord it over them, and their high officials exercise authority over them. Not so with you. Instead, whoever wants to become great among you must be your servant, and whoever wants to be first must be your slave—just as the Son of Man did not come to be served, but to serve, and to give his life as a ransom for many." (Matthew 10:25–28)

Jesus told his disciples that he would be executed like a criminal, dying on a cross. Simon Peter rebuked him (Mark 8:33)! Just before Jesus died, Peter said he would follow Jesus even to death (John 13:36–38). But he didn't keep his promise. When Jesus was arrested, Peter resorted to violent self-defense (John 18:1–11). When Jesus was tried before Pilate, Peter denied any association with Jesus three times (John 18:17, 25–27).

We too can be like Peter. We can follow Jesus, excited by his fishing miracles and the promise to become fishers of people. But when the way of Jesus starts to look like the way of service and suffering, suddenly we want to take the lead. Are we prepared to imitate Christ when it brings humiliation, pain, and even betrayal?

Risks and Rewards

 Read:

In the last session, we listened to passages throughout the Bible telling one story together. This time, let's look at how one Scripture passage can highlight several different themes. Ask three people designated "A," "B" and "C" to read parts of the text again and listen for the unique theme of each voice in the passage.

A: Luke 9:1–6
B: Luke 9:18–22
C: Luke 9:23–26
B: Luke 9:28–31, 44
C: Luke 9:57–62

What did each "voice" say about Jesus and what it means to follow him? (See my answers at the bottom of the next page.)

 Watch:

"I Have Decided to Follow Jesus"
(cbe.today/goodnews)

These lyrics were spoken by a Christian martyr in Northern India. The song later became popular during evangelical revivals in North America. In this video rendition, a modern Indian church depicts the story in a skit.

How does the story in the skit make you feel?

Take a moment to pray for the persecuted church today, then sing the song.

 Sing:

"I Have Decided to Follow Jesus" by Borivali Assembly
(cbe.today/goodnews)

I have decided to follow Jesus
I have decided to follow Jesus
I have decided to follow Jesus
I have decided to follow Jesus
No turning back, no turning back.

The world behind me, the cross before me
The world behind me, the cross before me
The world behind me, the cross before me
No turning back, no turning back

Though none go with me, still I will follow
Though none go with me, still I will follow

Though none go with me, still I will follow
No turning back, no turning back.

Membership in the Disciples Club

I've been saying "he" when talking about disciples, because all disciples of Jewish teachers were men. Jesus also chose twelve Jewish men as disciples. Some people say that this means today all church leaders should be men. It's true that because these men had been so close to Jesus, some of them became the first leaders of the early church. But remember, disciples were first and foremost followers of Jesus.

So why did Jesus choose twelve Jewish men as disciples? Twelve Jewish men symbolized the twelve tribes of Israel, who were named after Jacob's sons. Jesus was creating a new people of God and teaching them a new law.[4]

But Jesus also invited others to follow him. Voice A continues speaking in chapter 10. Ask voice A to read this passage:

📖 Read: Luke 10:1–3, 17

Cultural context: Why does Jesus appoint 72 or 70 others? The number 70 or 72 is the same number of nations that descended from Noah, listed in Genesis 10 (whether it was 70 or 72 depends on whether the translation was Greek or Hebrew).[5] It's a number that symbolizes universality—all nations, not just Jews.

Literary context: Jesus goes on to say that having Jewish heritage does not automatically lead to salvation. Jewish cities who rejected his message (Chorazin, Bethsaida, Capernaum) will be judged more harshly than the Gentile cities (Sodom, Tyre, and Sidon) because the Jews, who had been promised a Messiah, should have recognized him when he came (Luke 10:13–16).

The theme of voice A: Apostles are "sent ones." They heal, cast out demons, and preach the kingdom, just like their teacher.

B: Jesus is the Messiah. To fulfill the Law of Moses and the prophecies of people like Elijah, he must die in Jerusalem.

C: Disciples must be like their teacher. They must give up their homes, families, and lives to follow Jesus.

"The harvest is plentiful, but the workers are few," Jesus says, so we need everyone to follow and make followers of Jesus. Jesus shocks the Jews, who have been God's chosen ones for hundreds of years. He says that only listening to and believing in God's message shows that you are part of God's people.

Jesus says that people follow him like sheep follow their shepherd: "his sheep follow him because they know his voice" (John 10:4). Many women and Gentiles behave like disciples—they listen. Jesus refers to these unconventional followers when he says, "I have other sheep that are not of this sheep pen. I must bring them also. They too will listen to my voice, and there shall be one flock and one shepherd" (John 10:16).

Jewish men were Jesus' first followers, just as Jacob and his twelve sons became the first nation chosen by God. But Luke points out that people of other nations, and women are also called to be disciples. Let's look at what happens next in the chapter.

Mary of Bethany: Learn like a Disciple

Read: Luke 10:38–42

At the end of Luke 10, Mary sits at Jesus' feet, listening to his teachings. What did this action mean in its **cultural context**? Where I grew up in East Africa, women and children traditionally prepare food in the kitchen and serve it to the men and guests. After the men and guests are served, the women and children eat in the kitchen. If there is meat, the men choose the best pieces first, and the women and children eat the leftovers. I imagine this was also the case in Jesus' culture.

But Mary decided not to stay in the kitchen. She did something that women were not allowed to do. She sat at the feet of the teacher to listen to him. In Jesus' time, to sit at a teacher's feet meant you were a disciple of that teacher.[6] In other words, Mary chose to become Jesus' disciple, and Luke highlighted her decision. Her sister Martha couldn't believe it. Maybe she thought, "What will the neighbors think? What will the family think? Who will marry Mary now?"[7] But when Mary chose to follow Jesus rather than her culture's ideal for women, Jesus affirmed that she had chosen what was better.[8]

To try to imagine how shocking Mary's action would have been, picture a board meeting of a prestigious university. Men in expensive suits sit in a conference room discussing the future of education. The waitress serving coffee pulls up a chair at the table. The President of the university smiles and says, "Welcome. I'm glad you joined us. Colleagues, I'd like to introduce Mary, the newest member of the board."

Could Women be Disciples?

Mary of Bethany was not the only woman who followed Jesus (Luke 8:1–3). Jesus seemed to be opening the way for women to learn the law as well as men. But was this also true in the early church?

We know that Paul also advocated for women to learn theology, preparing them as teachers, preachers and evangelists. As we discussed in session 4, Paul affirmed that women "should learn in quietness and full submission," taking the humble posture of disciples alongside the men (1 Tim. 2:11). But what about the passage where Paul says that women should be silent in church and ask their husbands questions at home? Did women disciples need to be legitimized by their husbands to be students of the truth?

 Read: 1 Corinthians 14:26–35

Let's look at some **literary context** for this passage. In this section of the letter, Paul gives instructions on church order, using the same Greek word for "keeping quiet" three times:[9]

Who should stop talking?	When?	Why?
People who speak in tongues	If no interpreters are present	To build up the church (v.26) through peaceful (v.33) instruction and encouragement (v.31).
Prophets	If someone else has a message	
Women	Until after the service	

Clearly, prophets and tongues speakers were allowed to speak sometimes, but Paul also instructed them to be quiet sometimes—for the good of the assembly. In the same

Curious about why women were chatting? **Dig deeper** at the back of the book.

way, Paul does not restrict women from ever speaking in church gatherings. He gave instructions on how they should pray and prophesy only chapters before (1 Cor. 11). So in this case, the women must have been talking disruptively.

Our knowledge of the Corinthian **cultural context** suggests that the women were mostly uneducated and unable to understand what was going on, so they were probably asking their neighbor what was happening or chatting about unrelated subjects and drowning out the speaker.[10]

For the sake of everyone who wanted to learn, Paul offers instructions on how women can actively learn without interrupting others' learning. Asking questions afterward was a sign of taking initiative in one's learning—the Twelve asked Jesus questions in private after he had preached to the masses (Matt. 13:10, Mark 10:10).

Mary of Bethany: Love like a disciple

Let's shift our focus back to Mary of Bethany. She showed her willingness to learn like a disciple, but did she understand the commitment involved in following Jesus—even in service and suffering?

Before Jesus died, he visited the home of Martha and Mary twice. The first time was just after their brother Lazarus had died. The sisters told Jesus that Lazarus was ill, but he stayed where he was three more days (John 11:3–6). When Jesus finally arrived, he met the sisters:

 Read: John 11:21–35, 43–44

In summary: Martha told Mary, "The Teacher is here." Though Jewish teachers would not teach women, Martha and Mary knew Jesus as their teacher. People in Judea wanted to kill Jesus, but he risked his safety to visit these sisters, knowing he would eventually be killed by the people anyway.

Before he died he taught Martha and Mary that he was the resurrection and the life—in words (vv. 25–27), then in action (vv. 38–44).

In the next chapter, John records Jesus' final visit to Bethany, the week before his death. Returning again to the feet of Jesus, Mary performed the ultimate act of a disciple: self-sacrifice. She unbound her hair—sacrificing her image as a respectable woman. She poured a pint of pure nard on his feet—sacrificing a year's wages (John 12:3–5). She washed his feet like a servant—sacrificing her pride.

Jesus instructed his disciples to give up everything to follow him. Knowing that Jesus had risked his safety to visit her at Lazarus' death, Mary risked her reputation and income to prepare Jesus for his death.

Followers and Sent Ones

 Watch:

"Come Die with Me (feat. Propaganda)"
(cbe.today/goodnews)

Jesus instructed his disciples to take up their crosses and follow him. They ran away (Matt. 26:56). Of the Twelve, only John watched Jesus die. But the women followed Jesus to the cross.

> Many women were there, watching from a distance. They had followed Jesus from Galilee to care for his needs. Among them were Mary Magdalene, Mary the mother of James and Joseph, and the mother of Zebedee's sons. (Matthew 27:55–56)

After Jesus died, these women went to prepare his body for burial. When they arrived at the tomb, they discovered that Christ had risen from the dead. The angel told the group of women that Jesus was alive and sent them to tell the apostles the good news (Matt. 28:5–7). Since apostle means "sent one," the angel's instruction made the women apostles too.[11]

In John's gospel, Jesus finds Mary Magdalene in the garden. When she recognizes him, she says "rabboni," meaning "my teacher."[12] By including this detail, John reveals that she too is Jesus' disciple.

Simon Peter: A Second Chance

Simon Peter also eventually committed to following Jesus even if it meant service and suffering.

After Jesus' death and resurrection, Peter returned to his fishing boat. But Jesus called him again, reminding Peter that his true calling was to fish for people.

 Read: John 21:1–19

In summary: To counter Peter's three denials, Jesus asks Peter three times, "Do you love me?" When Peter replies, "Yes," Jesus tells Peter to feed his sheep. He will be a leader. But then Jesus predicts that Peter will be led to his death—he will lead by following Jesus to the cross (v. 18). According to church tradition, Peter was crucified upside down because he did not consider himself worthy to die on a cross upright, as Jesus had. Jesus concludes with two final reminders to Peter: "Follow me" and "You must follow me" (vv. 19, 22).

 Discuss:

Which parts of Peter and Mary's stories do you identify with and why? How does Jesus' response to them make you feel?

Which would be more difficult for you—sitting at someone's feet to learn, washing someone else's feet, or allowing someone you respect to wash your feet?

Sent Ones

True leaders follow the Leader—Christ. True followers are sent out to produce more followers. Jesus' last words in Matthew commissioned his disciples to become apostles and teachers. The disciples had memorized his words, learned their Rabbi's teachings, and tried to imitate his behaviors. Now it was time for them to go out and teach their own cohorts of disciples:

 Read: Matthew 28:16–20

We are all called to follow Jesus like the disciples. Jesus also commissions all of us to become apostles, or "sent ones," and make more followers for Jesus.

Discuss:

Making followers begins with telling people about Jesus, but includes mentoring them and modeling how to be a Jesus follower in your own life. How could you help make followers of Jesus?

 Pray:

Jesus, you call us to follow you. What a privilege to be your disciples! Write your words on our hearts. Teach us to imitate your servant ways. We trust that you love us and that you are more precious than any sacrifice you ask of us. As you make us more like you, send us to make disciples of all nations.

 Challenge: Surrender

Before the next session, spend some time praying or journaling about what you are willing to give up in order to follow Jesus. What are you holding back and why? Or, have you ignored a command God wants you to follow or a person God wants you to love? Ask Jesus to help you trust that he is worth it and to help you surrender to him. You may want to symbolize your surrender by writing a blank check or by singing "I have decided to follow Jesus" again. Come back to the group ready to share how Jesus is calling you to deeper discipleship.

 Go:

Until we meet again, let us keep our eyes fixed on our leader Jesus, who endured the cross for the joy ahead.

 Learn more:

The Heavenly Man by Brother Yun and Paul Hattaway
Brother Yun, a Chinese house church leader, has been tortured and imprisoned for his faith. But when he tells his story, his joy in knowing Jesus and sharing the gospel overpowers all of his earthly troubles. The Scripture he memorized often helped him sense God's presence in the midst of persecution.

Miraculous Movements: How Hundreds of Thousands of Muslims Are Falling in Love with Jesus by Jerry Trousdale

When Muslims decide to follow Jesus, they may be rejected by their families and risk persecution. Yet thousands have become committed Christ followers. The most successful evangelism efforts address the suffering that converts may face rather than promising seekers a life of comfort and prosperity. Evangelists tell Muslims that following Jesus will be hard—but worth it. Trousdale challenges us to reframe evangelism as the first step of discipleship—inviting people to commitment with communities where transformation occurs.

Until We Have New Bodies

"Therefore, I urge you, brothers and sisters, in view of God's mercy, to offer your bodies as a living sacrifice, holy and pleasing to God—this is your true and proper worship. "
Romans 12:1

 Challenge Check-in:

Can you say last session's theme verse?

What is God inviting you to sacrifice in exchange for more radical discipleship?

Throughout these chapters, we have considered how to embody the gospel. Our bodies are the way we experience this world's pain and pleasure, sickness and healing. We measure the passage of time by our body's rhythms of sleeping, eating, and growing. Our sense of identity comes from the way we understand our bodies: our gender, race, abilities, and more.

But when we are resurrected, we will be given new bodies. We are not certain what characteristics our new bodies will have. We know that people from every nation, tribe, people, and language will worship God (Rev. 7:9). But will the nations themselves still exist? Or will they pass away with the seas, the old heaven, and the old earth (Rev. 21:1)? We know that we will be like the angels, who do not marry (Matt. 22:30). Does that mean gender will pass away too? We do not know.

Our focus will be on Christ's body—the church, wearing a white robe. At last our community will be united across history and space.

The only marriage that will matter will be the wedding feast of Christ and the church, his bride. The engagement has taken all of history, and the celebration will be eternal.

 Read: Revelation 21:1–14, 22–27, 22:1–5

Which themes from our sessions do you notice? (My answers are at the bottom of the next page)

Here but not yet

Jesus proclaimed that the kingdom has come near (Matt. 4:17) and is in our midst (Luke 17:21). Yet he also taught his disciples to pray, "your kingdom come" (Matt. 6:10). The kingdom of heaven is here in many ways, but it will not be fully realized until Jesus returns. We are free from sin's power, but we still sin, and our world still suffers under sin's effects. Jesus has conquered death, yet it still hurts when loved ones pass away. Jesus was the "firstborn from the dead" (Rev. 1:5) but we still wait for our final resurrection. We live in this tension of "here but not yet."[1]

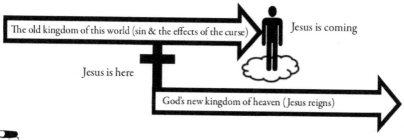

 Learn more:

Kingdom Come by Allen M. Wakabayashi

Accepting Christ as our Savior is only the beginning of our spiritual journey. Instead of saving only people's souls and waiting to escape to heaven, Jesus wants us to pray for God's kingdom to come on earth as it is in heaven—and then do something about it! If we believe that Jesus truly rules as king in this world and the next, how would we engage differently in the world's spiritual and social transformation?

Paul describes how our bodies feel the tension of the kingdom being here but not yet fully realized:

 Read: 2 Corinthians 4:6–5:20

What descriptions does Paul use to compare earthly and heavenly bodies?

What do you notice about the tension of the kingdom of being "here but not yet"?

How are we to live while in these bodies?

Although our resurrected bodies may or may not have a gender, for now we must ask ourselves: How will we embody the gospel as a community of ambassadors, male and female?

This is Not the End

 Discuss:

How have you grown in your understanding of God's Word through this study?

Do you see God any differently than when you began this study? Do you see yourself, the church, or others any differently? If so, how?

Think about the challenges you completed after each session. How have you grown in living out or embodying your faith?

Did any session especially impact you? Are there any areas where you sense that God may have more to say to you in the future?

Session 1: The Word's face is seen, and words are on his servants' foreheads (22:4).
Session 2: All nations gather in God's city (21:24–26). The victorious are called God's children and inherit a new heaven and earth (21:7).
Session 3: God dwells among the people—in a city even better than Jerusalem, the temple, or the tabernacle (21:3, 10, 22).
Session 4: There is no more pain (21:4) or curse (21:3). Eden is restored, and people eat from the tree of life (22:2–3).
Session 7: The city is built upon the foundations of the twelve tribes and the twelve apostles—God's followers (21:9–14).

As we end our sessions together, may this be the beginning of God doing a new work in and through our community.

The Word to the Body

 Explore, Pray and Go:

Let's pray using call and response. Many denominations practice liturgical prayer, where a leader reads something and the congregation responds in unison. Cultures without written song lyrics often sing call and response songs (where the leader and congregation each have different parts) or may have a leader sing each line in a song for the congregation to repeat.

In each session, we began with a theme verse to memorize and closed with a "go" call to action. To close our final session, we will put all these phrases together as our voices join together in prayer.

A "reader" will read the first memory verse, then pause. A few people can speak up with a word or phrase about what they are thankful for from that session. Then the reader will read the benediction, and the whole group will respond with the words in bold: "until we have new bodies." One person can be the reader throughout, or you can switch readers after each benediction.

The Word became flesh and made his dwelling among us. (John 1:14) [Pause for thanksgiving]

Let us seek to understand and live out God's word in our community... **until we have new bodies.**

There is neither Jew nor Gentile, neither slave nor free, nor is there male and female, for you are all one in Christ Jesus. If you belong to Christ, then you are Abraham's seed, and heirs according to the promise. (Galatians 3:28–29) [Pause for thanksgiving]

Let us cross barriers to unite as family under Jesus' name. . . **until we have new bodies.**

Don't you know that you yourselves are God's temple and that God's Spirit dwells in your midst? . . .[Y]ou together are that temple. (1 Corinthians 3:16–17) [Pause for thanksgiving]

Let us make the Spirit feel at home in our bodies and our community. . . **until we have new bodies.**

One of the teachers of the law [asked Jesus], "Of all of the commandments, which is the most important?"

"The most important one," answered Jesus, "is this: 'Hear, O Israel: The Lord our God, the Lord is one. Love the Lord your God with all your heart and with all your soul and with all your mind and with all your strength.' The second is this: 'Love your neighbor as yourself.' There is no commandment greater than these." (Mark 12:28–31) [Pause for thanksgiving]

Let us give thanks for God and each other, our allies in renewing creation. . . **until we have new bodies.**

Submit to one another out of reverence for Christ. (Ephesians 5:21) [Pause for thanksgiving]

Let us humbly love and serve other parts of the body. . . **until we have new bodies.**

Speaking the truth in love, we will grow to become in every respect the mature body of him who is the head, that is, Christ. From him the whole body, joined and held together by every supporting ligament, grows and builds itself up in love, as each part does its work. (Ephesians 4:15–16) [Pause for thanksgiving]

Let us build each other up in the church. . . **until we have new bodies.**

Whoever wants to be my disciple must deny themselves and take up their cross daily and follow me. (Luke 9:23) [Pause for thanksgiving]

Let us keep our eyes fixed on our leader Jesus, who endured the cross for the joy ahead... **until we have new bodies.**

Therefore, I urge you, brothers and sisters, in view of God's mercy, to offer your bodies as a living sacrifice, holy and pleasing to God—this is your true and proper worship. (Romans 12:1)

Let us offer our bodies to God in worship...**until we have new bodies.**

 Sing:

"Take My Life and Let It Be"
Words by Frances R. Havergal, 1874
Music by Henri Abraham Cesar Malan, 1827
Chris Tomlin's version (cbe.today/goodnews)

Take my life and let it be
consecrated, Lord, to Thee.
Take my moments and my days;
let them flow in ceaseless praise,
let them flow in ceaseless praise.

Take my hands, and let them move
at the impulse of Thy love.
Take my feet, and let them be
swift and beautiful for Thee,
swift and beautiful for Thee.

Take my voice, and let me sing
always, only, for my King.
Take my lips, and let them be
filled with messages from Thee,
filled with messages from Thee.

Take my silver and my gold;
not a mite would I withhold.
Take my intellect, and use
every power as Thou shalt choose,
every power as Thou shalt choose.

Take my will, and make it Thine;
it shall be no longer mine.
Take my heart, it is Thine own;
it shall be Thy royal throne,
it shall be Thy royal throne.

Take my love, my Lord, I pour
at Thy feet its treasure store.
Take myself, and I will be
ever, only, all for Thee,
ever, only, all for Thee.

 Challenge: Share your spiritual growth

This week, act as Christ's ambassador. Share what you learned through *Good News about Gender*. Talk to three people: a close friend, a mentor, and someone of a different faith. Go forth from this group ready to embody God's Word together.

DIG DEEPER
In-Depth Study Resources

This section provides in-depth interpretation of difficult passages for people to read before the relevant sessions.

Depending on your group, either:

a group leader can read through these so that they are prepared to answer questions, or

if your group is intellectually curious, everyone can read these beforehand and come prepared for discussion.

Session 2: Adopted Children with an Inheritance

 Watch:

"Biblical Basis for Women's Service in the Church" by N.T. Wright (cbe.today/goodnews)

Watch from 0:00 to 6:00 to hear how Galatians 3 does not erase the gender distinctions, but affirms that both men and women have equal inheritance in God's family.

Session 4: God's True Image

 Learn more:

"The Bible Teaches the Equal Standing of Men and Women" by Philip B. Payne (cbe.today/goodnews)

Using examples from the Old Testament, Jesus' ministry and Paul's letters, Philip B. Payne shows how Scripture supports the equal standing of men and women. He also analyzes the cultural, historical, and literary context of passages that seem to forbid women from being in ministry.

Session 5: Powerful Love in the Body

How does Ephesians 5 compare with what Aristotle says in his household code? Aristotle's code says:

> Of household management we have seen that there are three parts- one is the rule of a master over slaves. . . another of a father, and the third of a husband. A husband and father, we saw, rules over wife and children, both free, but the rule differs, the rule over his children being a royal, over his wife a constitutional rule. For although there may be exceptions to the order of nature, the male is by nature fitter for command than the female, just as the elder and full-grown is superior to the younger and more immature. . .
>
> The freeman rules over the slave after another manner from that in which the male rules over the female, or the man over

the child; although the parts of the soul are present in all of them, they are present in different degrees. For the slave has no deliberative faculty at all; the woman has, but it is without authority, and the child has, but it is immature. So it must necessarily be supposed to be with the moral virtues also; all may be supposed to partake of them, but only in such manner and degree as is required by each for the fulfillment of his duty.[1]

Session 6: Build the Body

New Testament scholar Philip Payne offers one of the most compelling interpretations of 1 Corinthians 11. Here is a summary.[2]

Cultural & historical context: What were the head coverings and why did they matter?

Although some interpretations of 1 Corinthians 11 suggest that women should cover their heads with veils, art from Paul's day shows that respectable women in Greek and Roman cities usually wore their hair done up on their heads as a "covering."[3] Paul also speaks against women who braid their hair with gold (1 Tim. 2:9, 1 Pet. 3:3), suggesting that women's hair was visible, not veiled.

Both Greek and Jewish men wore their hair short and uncovered.[4]

Corinth was a religious center. One of her many temples hosted the Dionysiac cult—a group known for wild sexual revelry. In the Dionysiac cult, women let their hair loose to prophesy, symbolically throwing off the constraints of marriage.[5] Men in this cult grew their hair long in an effeminate style that signaled availability for homosexual revelry.

Since Paul appeals to the Corinthians' own judgment (11:13), he is not introducing a new custom.[6] This suggests that the head coverings Paul refers to are hair. He's encouraging women to cover their heads by doing their hair up respectably, and men not to cover their head with long effeminate hair. Paul says that an uncovered woman is "one and the same as the shaved woman" (1 Cor. 11:5, Payne's literal translation), implying that there is a specific shaved woman he is referring to. In Paul's day, adulteresses were punished by shaving their heads, to make them hang their heads in obvious shame.[7]

It may seem strange that people leading prayer and prophesy in the church would wear hairstyles like worshippers in a sexual cult, but we know that the Corinthian church absorbed the city's loose attitude toward sexual immorality. They were even justifying the behavior of a church members who committed incest and had sex with prostitutes, arguing that their freedom in Christ gave them the right to do these things (1 Cor. 5, 6:12–20).

Logic: Does head really mean "source"?

To Paul, the Corinthians' inappropriate dress and behavior in worship were a result of failing to understand the relationship between God, men, and women. For this reason, Paul provides a theological explanation for his request that the Corinthians wear appropriate hairstyles. In the session, we talk about how "head" often meant the origin or source of something in Paul's day. But how do we know that's what it meant in this passage?

Supposing Paul were using "head" to mean authority, the passage would seem to create a hierarchy of authority of God over Christ, Christ over men, and men over women. But notice that Paul does not list these pairs in a logical sequence related to power or authority. Instead, he structures his sentence: man-Christ, woman-man, Christ-God.[8]

It is odd that Paul would suggest Christ has authority over man, so that woman would experience Christ's authority indirectly—through her husband. Christ's death ended the need for a human (the high priest) to mediate the relationship between God and humanity (Heb. 9:15).

If the hierarchy were a logical progression of authority, you would expect the difference between each level of authority to be roughly equal. But while man and woman are both human, and God and Christ are both God, there is a big gap between Christ and man.[9] If the Christ-man and

God-Christ relationships had parallel structures of authority, God the Son would be permanently subjugated to God the Father—an unacceptable conclusion. In fact, the notion that God the Son is eternally subordinate to God the Father is a heresy called Arianism, which the church denounced at the First Council of Nicea in AD 325, and solidified in the Nicene Creed.[10] And how could the difference between Christ and man be the same as the difference between man and woman—two humans?[11]

If for Paul head meant source, we see that his sentence order is chronological. Adam came into the world through Christ (through whom all things were created—Col. 1:16), then Eve came into the world from Adam's body, then Christ came into the world incarnate sent from God.[12]

Literary Structure: We Need Each Other

Paul's structure actually demonstrates balance, not hierarchy. He uses a common biblical literary technique called a chiasmus, which has the shape of the Greek letter X. It's a structure where pairs of similar ideas are placed before and after the main point as a symmetrical frame for the main idea, to highlight its importance. Below, I've color-coded the framing pairs to illustrate Paul's central point in this passage:[13]

Paul's structure also draws attention to the center of his argument: "It is for this reason that a woman ought to have authority over her own head, because of the angels" (1 Cor. 11:10). Scholars disagree about what the angels may mean in this passage.[14] Either way, Paul is saying that women have authority themselves. They are already praying and prophesying in the meetings. Covering their head with their hair enables them to exercise that authority without looking like indecent cult worshippers and therefore bringing shame and dishonor on themselves.

A - Regarding the traditions: Christ is the head of man, man the head of woman, and God the head of Christ.

B - A man who prays or prophesies with his head covered dishonors his head, while a woman who prays or prophesies with her head uncovered dishonors her head.

C - Man is the image and glory of God, and woman the glory of man. Woman came from man, and was made for man.

D - For this reason a woman ought to have authority over her own head, because of the angels.

C - But in the Lord women and men are not independent. Woman came from man, and man comes from woman - and everything comes from God.

B - A woman should cover her head when praying. Nature shows that a man's long hair is disgraceful, but a woman's long hair is her covering.

A - We have no other practice - nor do the churches of God

Session 7: Follow and Make Followers

Kenneth E. Bailey grew up in the Middle East and studies the cultural world of the Bible. He describes a situation that he believes might be similar to the situation Paul was addressing:

> I have preached in village churches in Egypt where the women were seated on one side of the church and the men on the other. There was a wooden partition about six feet high separating the two sections. I preached in simple colloquial Arabic, but the women were often illiterate and the preacher was expected to preach for at least an hour—and we had problems. The women quickly passed the limit of their attention span. The children were seated with them

and chatting inevitably broke out among the women. The chatting would at times become so loud that no one could hear the preacher. (These villages had no electricity and no sound amplification.) One of the senior elders would stand up and in a desperate voice shout, "Let the women be silent in the church!" and we would proceed. After about ten minutes the scene would repeat.[15]

John Chrysostom experienced the same problem when trying to preach in the fourth century in the cathedral in Antioch—the women would chat as if they were in a market. Explaining the utility of Paul's advice, he said, "unless they are quiet, they cannot learn anything that is useful. For when our discourse [sermon] strains against the talking, and no one minds what is said, what good can it do to them?"[16]

The same situation was likely the problem in Corinth. Since Corinth was an international trading hub and Greece's largest city, the Corinthian church may have been comprised of people from various backgrounds, whose only common language was Greek. While men probably had the chance to gain fluency in Greek from their work, and could understand different accents, women likely only spoke enough Greek for their basic needs. With no formal schooling, these women were also unaccustomed to sitting and listening for hours. As their attention wandered, they may have asked their neighbor to explain what was said or begin chatting about other subjects.[17]

Activity and Resource Summary

By Chapter

Session 1: The Word & the Body
Theme Verse: John 1:14
Main texts: Psalm 33, John 1
Explore: Write a song / make words with your body
Watch: Studio C "Prop Switch"
Sing: Your own song
Challenge: Memorize the theme verse
Learn more: *How to Read the Bible for All Its Worth*; *The Blue Parakeet*
Dig Deeper: None

Session 2: Adopted Children with an Inheritance
Theme Verse: Gal. 3:28
Main texts: Gen. 15, 17, Matt. 1
Explore: Monopoly story; Game Show of Jesus' lineage
Watch: Sinach "I Know Who I Am"
Sing: Be Thou My Vision
Challenge: Learn about the global church
Learn more: Christian for Biblical Equality (CBE) website;
Kingdom without Borders
Dig Deeper: Lecture Clip by N. T. Wright: "Biblical Basis for
Women's Service in the Church"

Session 3: Priests & God's Temple

Theme Verse: 1 Cor. 3:16-17
Main texts: Heb. 9-10, Acts 2, 1 Peter 2
Explore: Images of places of worship
Watch: Hannah Rasmussen "Holy Week Women"
Sing: Jesus at the Center of it All
Challenge: Silent retreat
Learn more: *Jesus Have I Loved, But Paul?*; *Women Called to Witness*
Dig Deeper: None

Session 4: Created Allies

Theme Verse: Mark 12:28-31
Main texts: Gen. 2-3 & 1 Tim. 2
Explore: Lists traits of men, women & God
Watch: FTE "Love God, Love Neighbor"
Sing: Build Your Kingdom Here
Challenge: The prayer of examen
Learn more: *Half the Sky*; *Half the Church*
Dig Deeper: Footnotes and Payne's article

Session 5: Powerful Love in the Body

Theme Verse: Eph. 5:21
Main texts: Eph. 5
Explore: Talk about remixes / parodies
Watch: Any parody video
Sing: The Servant Song
Challenge: Use your power to serve
Learn more: *The Red Letter Revolution*
Dig Deeper: Aristotle's Household Code

Session 6: Build the Body

Theme Verse: Eph. 4:15-16
Main texts: 1 Cor. 11-12, Eph. 4, Rom. 12
Explore: Present spiritual gifts
Watch: Juanita Bynum "I Need You to Survive"

Sing: I Need you to Survive
Challenge: Seek out a mentor
Learn more: *Creating a Missional Culture*, *Equipped for Every Good Work*
Dig Deeper: Compiled research on 1 Cor. 11

Session 7: Follow & Make Followers

Theme Verse: Luke 9:23
Main texts: 1 Cor. 14, Luke 9-10, John 11, John 21
Explore: Imitate a famous person
Watch: Propaganda "Come Die with Me"
Sing: I Have Decided to Follow Jesus
Challenge: Surrender
Learn more: *The Heavenly Man*; *Miraculous Movements*
Dig Deeper: Kenneth Bailey's explanation for 1 Cor. 14

Session 8: Until We Have New Bodies

Theme Verse: Rom. 12:1-2
Main texts: 2 Cor. 4-5
Explore: Call and Response prayer
Watch: None
Sing: Take My Life and Let It Be
Challenge: Tell someone about what you learned
Learn more: *Kingdom Come*
Dig Deeper: None

By Activity

" " Theme Verse

Session 1: John 1:14
Session 2: Gal. 3:28-29
Session 3: 1 Cor. 3:16-17
Session 4: Mark 12:28-31
Session 5: Eph. 5:21
Session6: Eph. 4:15-16
Session 7: Luke 9:23
Session 8: Rom. 12:1-2

📖 **Main Texts**

Session 1: Psalm 33, John 1
Session 2: Gen. 15, 17, Matt. 1
Session 3: Heb. 9-10, Acts 2, 1 Peter 2
Session 4: Gen. 2-3 & 1 Tim. 2
Session 5: Eph. 5
Session 6: 1 Cor. 11-12, Eph. 4, Rom. 12
Session 7: 1 Cor. 14, Luke 9-10, John 11, John 21
Session 8: 2 Cor. 4-5

🔍 **Explore**

Session 1: Write a song / make words with your body
Session 2: Monopoly story; Game Show of Jesus' lineage
Session 3: Images of places of worship
Session 4: Lists traits of men, women & God
Session 5: Talk about remixes / parodies
Session 6: Present spiritual gifts
Session 7: 1 Cor. 14, Luke 9-10, John 11, John 21
Session 8: Call and Response prayer

🎬 **Watch**

Session 1: Studio C "Prop Switch"
Session 2: Sinach "I Know Who I Am"
Session 3: Hannah Rasmussen "Holy Week Women
Session 4: FTE "Love God, Love Neighbor"
Session 5: Any parody video
Session 6: Juanita Bynum "I Need You to Survive"
Session 7: Propaganda "Come Die with Me"
Session 8: None

🎵 **Sing**

Session 1: Your own song
Session 2: Be Thou My Vision
Session 3: Jesus at the Center of it All
Session 4: Build Your Kingdom Here

Session 5: The Servant Song
Session 6: I Need you to Survive
Session 7: I Have Decided to Follow Jesus
Session 8: Take My Life and Let It Be

🏆 Challenge
Session 1: Memorize the theme verse
Session 2: Learn about the global church
Session 3: Silent retreat
Session 4: The prayer of examen
Session 5: Use your power to serve
Session 6: Seek out a mentor
Session 7: Surrender
Session 8: Tell someone about what you learned

📚 Learn More
Session 1: *How to Read the Bible for All Its Worth*; *The Blue Parakeet*
Session 2: Christians for Biblical Equality (CBE) website;
Kingdom without Borders
Session 3: *Jesus Have I Loved, But Paul?*; *Women Called to Witness*
Session 4: *Half the Sky*; *Half the Church*
Session 5: *The Red Letter Revolution*
Session 6: *Creating a Missional Culture*; *Equipped for Every Good Work*
Session 7: *The Heavenly Man*; *Miraculous Movements*
Session 8: *Kingdom Come*

🧗 Dig Deeper
Session 1: None
Session 2: Lecture Clip by N. T. Wright: "Biblical Basis for Women's Service in the Church"
Session 3: None
Session 4: Footnotes and Payne's article
Session 5: Aristotle's Household Code
Session 6: Compiled research on 1 Cor. 11
Session 7: Kenneth Bailey's explanation for 1 Cor. 14
Session 8: None

Notes

Session 1: Living Word

1. Henry Blackaby, Richard Blackaby, and Claude King, *Experiencing God: Knowing and Doing the Will of God*, 2nd ed. (Nashville: B & H Books, 2008), 57.

2. Psalm 133 set to music in its original Hebrew: http://youtu.be/lZs9ld3klPo; U2's version of Psalm 40: http://youtu.be/1XzHlySYR_Y; The Brooklyn Tabernacle choir singing Psalm 3: http://youtu.be/MybjSe_WWn4 "10,000 Reasons," which is Matt Redman's version of Psalm 103: http://youtu.be/XtwIT8JjddM.

3. A great resource to learn about exegesis and hermeneutics is Gordon D. Fee and Douglas Stuart's book, *How to Read the Bible for all Its Worth*, 4th ed. (Grand Rapids: Zondervan, 2014).

4. See the note on Matt. 26:23 in Walter W. Wessel and Ralph Earle, "Matthew" in *The NIV Study Bible, 2011*, ed. Kenneth L. Barker (Grand Rapids: Zondervan, 2011), 1641.

5. The concept of the Bible as a play and Christian life as acting out the playwright's will comes from Stephen C. Barton, *Life Together: Family, Sexuality and Community in the New Testament and Today* (Edinburgh: T & T Clark, 2001).

6. The dignity that God's incarnation gave to the human body is an idea that comes from a remote tribe in Northern Kenya. Harold Miller, in discussion with the author, February 2015.

Session 2: Adopted Children with an Inheritance

1. This way of looking at Israel's inheritance laws and the Monopoly activity from Steven Rasmussen. Inspired by Peter Kimuru, "Session 5: Moral Basis for Land Ownership and Distribution" (Kenya, 2012) 31–24, Published in a brochure for the conference "Regional Land Context for Peaceful Co-existence in Kenya," 2012.

2. Scripture records the firstborn's double inheritance (Deut. 21:15–17), cases where daughters inherit (Num. 27:1–8; 36:1–12), and the importance of land staying within the tribe (Num. 36:7).

3. See the note on Gen. 15:17 in Ronald F. Youngblood, "Genesis" in *The NIV Study Bible, 2011*, ed. Kenneth L. Barker (Grand Rapids: Zondervan, 2011), 35

4. See the note on Gen. 17:10 in ibid., 37.

5. See Raymond Dillard, "Introduction: 1 Chronicles" in *The NIV Study Bible, 2011*, ed. Kenneth L. Barker (Grand Rapids: Zondervan, 2011), 627-628 .

6. Gordon D. Fee, "Male and Female in the New Creation" in *Discovering Biblical Equality: Complementarity without Hierarchy*, 2nd ed., eds. Ronald W. Pierce, Rebecca Merrill Groothuis, and Gordon D. Fee (Downers Grove, IL: IVP Academic, 2005), 180.

7. J. R. Daniel Kirk, *Jesus Have I Loved, but Paul?: A Narrative Approach to the Problem of Pauline Christianity* (Grand Rapids: Baker Academic, 2011), 62.

Session 3: Priests and God's Temple

1. See diagrams "Zerubbabel's Temple" and "Herod's Temple" in *The NIV Study Bible, 2011*, ed. Kenneth L. Barker (Grand Rapids: Zondervan, 2011), 729, 1596.

2. Mark Levitt and John Parsons, "The Jewish Holidays: A Simplified Overview of the Feasts of the Lord," Hebrew4Christians, accessed April 7, 2016, http://www.hebrew4christians.com/Holidays/Introduction/introduction.html. On this webpage, Messianic Jews explain how the Jewish holidays in Leviticus 23 were fulfilled in Jesus' life, death, and resurrection, as well as in the birth of the church at Pentecost.

3. Concept from Robert Boyd Munger, *My Heart - Christ's Home*, 2nd ed. (Downers Grove, IL: IVP Books, 1986).

Session 4: Created Allies

1. The NIV 2011 translation here calls human beings "mankind" to show the connection between the Adam and humanity, but since "mankind" sounds strangely masculine without the context of the Hebrew word, I used the NLT's "human beings" version in this instance. In session 6, I will use the NIV 2011 in order to make a point.

2. Our male and femaleness is not a way that we reflect God's image uniquely. Animals and plants are male and female. N. T. Wright makes this point in "The Biblical Basis for Women's Service in the Church," *Priscilla Papers* 20, no. 4 (Autumn 2006): 5–10.

3. The material in this paragraph comes from Carolyn Custis James, *Half the Church: Recapturing God's Global Vision for Women* (Grand Rapids: Zondervan, 2011), 112.

4. See the note on Rev 12:10 in Robert Mounce and Andrew J. Bandstra, "Revelation" in *The NIV Study Bible, 2011*, ed. Kenneth L. Barker (Grand Rapids: Zondervan, 2011), 2165.

5. Elsewhere in the Bible, we see that listening to the counsel of women who do not fear God (like Delilah and Jezebel) leads men into serious trouble. However, listening to godly women (like Ruth and Esther) turns out for the salvation of a people. God told Abraham to listen to Sarah, and Abigail's initiative softened David's anger against her husband Nabal. Overall, listening to and obeying God is what counts—and sometimes God speaks through people.

6. Unless otherwise mentioned, content in this section comes from Philip B. Payne, *Man and Woman, One in Christ*. (Grand Rapids: Zondervan, 2009).

7. Along with Paul's focus on false teaching, this letter also talks more about women than most of the New Testament. See Linda Belleville, "Teaching and Usurping Authority," in *Discovering Biblical Equality*, 2nd ed., eds. Ronald W. Pierce, Rebecca Merrill Groothuis, and Gordon D. Fee (Downers Gorve, IL: IVP Academic 2005).

8. Loren Cunningham, David Joel Hamilton, and Janice Rogers. *Why not Women? A Biblical Study of Women in Missions, Ministry, and Leadership*. (Seattle: YWAM Publishing, 2000), 217–218.

9. Ibid.

10. Unless otherwise mentioned, content in this section comes from Payne, *Man and Woman, One in Christ*.

11. Some people generalize the statement, saying that women are more prone to deception than men. Taken to its logical conclusion, that would mean men are never the ones deceived—which we know from experience is not true. If Adam ate from the tree without being deceived at all, he sinned willfully, making him even less trustworthy than his wife. We know Eve gave Adam the fruit and he listened to her, and "then the eyes of both of them were opened" (Gen. 3:6, 7, 17). So it's more likely that Paul meant that "Adam was not the one deceived" by the snake specifically. The snake was the first false teacher, and Eve his first prey. See Payne, *Man and*

Woman, One in Christ, 392.

12. Some people interpret "the childbirth" to mean the process of labor. It makes no sense that women's spiritual salvation would be dependent on their motherhood, especially with Paul's emphasis on faith over works. So some people say this verse means that godly women will be kept safe while giving labor. But this creates a strange victim-blaming situation, where Christian women who miscarry or die in labor must not have had enough faith, love, or holiness. And, of course, some women never have children.

As we noted in our exercise, Paul uses the word "saved" in a spiritual context earlier in the chapter. The Greek word for "childbirth" refers to an event, not the process of labor. Many church fathers referred to Jesus' birth as "THE" childbirth, as Paul does here. After describing the fall, Paul references its effects in Genesis 3, where God increases Eve's pains in childbearing, but promises her that one day, the woman's seed will crush the snake's head (3:15–16). Isaiah foretold the significance of the virgin who would "give birth to a son" (Is. 7:14, 9:6). The same language is repeated multiple times when announcing Jesus' birth (Luke 1:31, 1:42, 2:11–12). Paul is offering hope for women. Even though some of them have been deceived, Eve's promise has been fulfilled. If they continue in faith, love, and holiness, they will be saved, because Jesus has crushed the deceiver.

13. I see interesting parallels between Paul's instructions to Timothy about Ephesus and his letter directly to the Ephesian church (Eph. 4:1–16). Adam failed to recognize Eve as God's gift to him. Paul explains that Christ has given us to each other as gifts to build each other up. Eve wanted to have God's knowledge, but she was deceived. Paul explains that the church together will achieve full knowledge of God and be free of deception. Instead of promoting oneself and usurping authority in order to spread false teaching, the church must speak the truth in love.

14. Unless otherwise mentioned, the following examples are taken from McKnight, *The Blue Parakeet*, 178–185.

15. Kirk, *Jesus Have I Loved, but Paul?*, 123–125.

Session 5: Powerful Love in the Body

1. This argument comes from I. Howard Marshall, "Mutual Love and Submission in Marriage" in *Discovering Biblical Equality*, 2nd ed.

2. For more detailed explanation of the cultural context, see "The Cultural Context of Ephesians 5:18–6:9" by Gordon D. Fee in *Priscilla Papers* 16, no. 1 (Winter 2002): 3–7. Accessible online at: http://www.cbeinternational.org/resources/article/priscilla-papers/cultural-context-ephesians-518–69. Hear his lecture on the topic: http://youtu.be/6NGhHU0h1RM?list=PL1A120A7FB0830B1F.

3. Marshall, "Mutual Love and Submission in Marriage" in *Discovering Biblical Equality*, 199.

4. Fee, "The Cultural Context of Ephesians 5:18–6:9."

5. Rachel Held Evans, "Aristotle vs. Jesus: What Makes the New Testament Household Codes Different" *Rachel Held Evans* (blog), August 28, 2013, http://rachelheldevans.com/blog/aristotle-vs-jesus-what-makes-the-new-testament-household-codes-different.

6. Fee, "The Cultural Context of Ephesians 5:18–6:9."

7. Marshall, "Mutual Love and Submission in Marriage" in *Discovering Biblical Equality*, 191.

8. Ibid., 197.

9. Gal. 5:13, as translated by Marshall, ibid.

10. In democratic societies, how we submit to political authority may be different than Jews in the Roman Empire. Civilly disobedient activists, for instance, submit to authority's punishment in order to create a more just society. For more on Christian involvement in politics, check out Tony Campolo and Shane Claiborne's book, *Red Letter Revolution*, listed in the Learn More recommendation at the end of this chapter.

11. American sociologist Willard Waller, who studied family life, discovered that romantic partners often try to gain power over each other by withholding love. He called this the "principle of least interest." See Willard Walter Waller, *The Family: A Dynamic Interpretation* (Wilmington, MA: Holt, Rinehart and Winston, 1951). Cited in Tony Campolo, *Choose Love not Power: How to Right the World's Wrongs from a Place of Weakness* (Ventura, CA: Regal Books, 2009), 26–28.

Session 6: Build the Body

1. Payne, *Man and Woman, One in Christ*, 122–123.

2. Rev. 2:23 is translated in the NIV as "I am he who searches heart and minds" but the footnote in the NIV 2011 Study Bible says: "'Minds' [lit. 'kidneys'] probably refers here to the will and the affections; 'hearts' may designate the center of rational life." See the note on Rev 2:23 in Robert Mounce and Andrew J. Bandstra, "Revelation" in *The NIV Study Bible, 2011*, ed. Kenneth L. Barker (Grand Rapids: Zondervan, 2011), 2154.

3. For more in depth discussion of the meaning of "head," see Alan F. Johnson, "A Review of the Scholarly Debate on the Meaning of 'Head,' (κεφαλη) in Paul's Writings" *Ashland Theological Journal* 41 (2009), 35–57.

4. For instance, Payne mentions a famous saying about the Greek god Zeus which stated: "Zeus is the head, Zeus the middle, and from Zeus all things exist." The distinction between Jewish and Greek meanings of "head" comes from in Payne, *Man and Woman, One in Christ*, 117–128. Also see Gordon D. Fee, "Praying and Prophesying in the Assemblies: 1 Corinthians 11:2–16" in *Discovering Biblical Equality: Complementarity without Hierarchy*, 2nd ed. (Downers Grove, IL: IVP Academic, 2005) 150–151.

5. Kenneth E. Bailey, *Paul Through Mediterranean Eyes: Cultural Studies in 1 Corinthians* (Downers Grove, IL: IVP Academic, 2011), 302.

6. See the text notes on Gen 2:7 and 5:1-2 in Ronald F. Youngblood, "Genesis" in *The NIV Study Bible, 2011*, ed. Kenneth L. Barker (Grand Rapids: Zondervan, 2011), 14, 17.

7. I use the NIV 2011's translation, which is closer to the Hebrew, to connect Gen. 2:7, 5:1–2 and 1 Cor. 11:7. At this point in the creation story, Adam's name is synonymous with all of humanity. In chapter two, God takes Eve out of Adam's rib. You could interpret Genesis 1:27 as a chronological summary of the creation process—God creates humanity or "adam" (chapter one), then creates Eve, which creates the distinction between male and female (chapter two). There are other interpretations too. For instance, the two stories might describe male and female being created in the same breath versus in a more elaborate process because of the point they are trying to make: Genesis 1's focus is on the structure of the week—creation and Sabbath, whereas Genesis 2 focuses on the relationships between God, Adam, Eve, and the rest of creation. I owe the explanation of these concepts to Rabbi Barry Cytron's Hebrew Bible class at Macalester College, Saint Paul, MN.

8. Bailey, *Paul Through Mediterranean Eyes*, 307.

9. Payne, *Man and Woman, One in Christ*, 115.

10. Ibid., 179–181.

11. Ronald Pierce, *Partners in Marriage and Ministry: A Biblical Picture of Gender Equality. Christians for Biblical Equality* (Minneapolis, MN: Christians for Biblical Equality, 2011), 85.

12. Most of the explanation and examples below of each spiritual gift are based on Don and Katie Fortune, *Discover your God-given Gifts,* 2nd ed. (Grand Rapids: Chosen Books, 2009) and Paul R. Ford, *Unleash your Church* (Pasadena, CA: Charles E. Fuller Intitute, 1993).

Session 7: Follow and Make Followers

1. I searched the NIV 2011 for the word "lead" and the word "follow." There were lots of references in the Pentateuch to the God leading the Israelites out of Egypt, but the word "lead" was used as a command only three times (Ex. 32:34, Ex. 33:12, Deut. 10:11). The word "follow" usually was used in the context of God instructing the Israelites to follow the law and not to follow other gods—and this word was used over forty times!

2. D. Thomas Lancaster, *King of the Jews: Resurrecting the Jewish Jesus* (Marshfield, MO: First Fruits of Zion, 2006), 52–53. Find First Fruits of Zion online at www.ffoz.org.

3. Michael Wilkins, *Following the Master: A Biblical Theology of Discipleship* (Grand Rapids: Zondervan, 1992), 125.

4. Pierce, *Partners in Marriage and Ministry*, 32.

5. See the note on Luke 10:1 in Lewis Foster, "Luke" in *The NIV Study Bible, 2011*, ed. Kenneth L. Barker (Grand Rapids: Zondervan, 2011), 1725.

6. Kenneth E. Bailey, *Jesus Through Middle Eastern Eyes: Cultural Studies in the Gospels* (Downers Grove, IL: IVP Academic, 2008).

7. Ibid.

8. See study notes on Luke 10:39, 40, 42 in Mark Strauss, "Luke" in the *NLT Study Bible*, ed. Sean Harrison (Carol Stream, IL: Tyndale House Publishers, 2008).

9. The Greek word is σιγάω, written with the English alphabet as *sigaó*.

10. This information taken from Bailey, *Paul through Mediterranean Eyes*, 409–418.

11. McKnight, *The Blue Parakeet*, 178–185.

12. The only other person recorded calling Jesus this strengthened form of "rabbi" was blind Bartimaeus begging for healing in Mark 10:51. See the note on John 20:16 in Leon Morris, "John" in *The NIV Study Bible, 2011*, ed. Kenneth L. Barker (Grand Rapids: Zondervan, 2011), 1807.

Session 8: Until We Have New Bodies

1. These ideas are articulated in more detail in Allen M. Wakabayashi, *Kingdom Come: How Jesus Wants to Change the World* (Downers Grove, IL: IVP Books, 2003).

Dig Deeper

1. These ideas are articulated in more detail in Wakabayashi, *Kingdom Come*.

2. Unless otherwise mentioned, this section and the next are taken from Payne, *Man and Woman, One in Christ*.

3. Ibid., 152–162.

4. Ibid., 141–146.

5. Ibid., 162–164.

6. Ibid., 207–210.

7. Ibid., 172.

8. Pierce, *Partners in Marriage and Ministry*, 86–87.

9. Payne, *Man and Woman, One in Christ*, 129.

10. Roger E. Olson, *The Story of Christian Theology: Twenty Centuries of Tradition and Reform* (Downers Grove, IL: IVP, 1999), 151–160.

11. Homily 26 on 1 Cor. 11:2–16 from Talbot W. Chambers, "The Homilies of Saint John Chrysostom on the Epistles of Paul to the Corinthians" in *Nicene and Post-Nicene Fathers* (Grand Rapids: Eerdmans, 1979), 12:150–51).

12. Bailey, *Paul through Mediterranean Eyes*, 302.

13. Adapted from Pierce, *Partners in Marriage and Ministry*, 85.

14. Paul could be referring to the fact that angels cover their body parts in God's presence (Dachollom Datiri, "1 Corinthians" in in *The Africa Bible Commentary*, ed. Tokunboh Adeyemo [Grand Rapids: Zondervan, 2006], 1416), that angels were thought to assist in prophecy (Pierce, *Partners in Marriage and Ministry*), that gender differentiates humans but not angels (Fee, "Praying and Prophesying in the Assemblies: 1 Corinthians 11:2–16" in *Discovering Biblical Equality*), or that angels observe worship and report to God (Payne, *Man and Woman, One in Christ*). Whatever the case may be, the point seems to be that women should not bring shame to their heads by acting indecently and letting down their hair.

15. Bailey, *Paul through Mediterranean Eyes*, 414.

16. Chrysostom, "Homily IX [I Timothy ii, 11–15]," in *Nicene and Post-Nicene Fathers* (Grand Rapids: Eerdmans, 1979), 13:435. Cited in Bailey, *Paul through Mediterranean Eyes*, 415.

17. Bailey, *Paul through Mediterranean Eyes*, 409–418.